Step Up to INTERMEDIATE
Math

Three Levels of Learning!

Carson-Dellosa Publishing Company, Inc. • Greensboro, North Carolina

Credits

Editor: Barrie Hoople

Layout Design: Lori Jackson

Inside Illustrations: Lori Jackson and Bill Neville

Cover Design: Lori Jackson

Cover Photo: © 1997 Comstock, Inc.

This book has been correlated to state, national, and Canadian provincial standards. Visit *www.carsondellosa.com* to search for and view its correlations to your standards.

ISBN: 978-1-60022-975-6

Table of Contents

Purpose

In any classroom, there are students who are working above and below grade level. These varying readiness levels present a daily challenge as teachers strive to meet the needs of every student. By differentiating instruction, teachers can provide modifications to meet these varying student needs. *Step Up to Math: Intermediate* is a practical tool that teachers can use to help differentiate instruction and reinforce core skills.

What Is Differentiated Instruction?

Differentiated instruction is a term used to describe an educational methodology that modifies instruction to accommodate the needs of individual students. These modifications involve offering multiple approaches to content, instruction, and assessment. Since students have varying ability levels, differentiation allows all students to maximize their strengths. Challenging and supporting all students through differentiated instruction results in increased motivation and student learning.

How Can Educators Effectively Differentiate Instruction?

Acknowledging that children learn in different ways is the first step toward differentiating instruction. Below are specific suggestions for differentiating instruction in the classroom:

1. Offer multiple methods for students to demonstrate success.

2. Provide a variety of materials at various levels that address various learning styles.

3. Tailor assignments to meet students' needs.

4. Provide appropriate learning experiences for all students.

5. Allow each student to work at his or her individual pace.

6. Support students by giving help as needed.

7. Provide learning tasks at an appropriate level of difficulty.

Step Up to Math: Intermediate provides learning activities that offer students opportunities to develop needed skills and demonstrate individual strengths.

In This Book

Step Up to Math: Intermediate is divided into core skills within each subject area. A detailed Table of Contents helps teachers identify and choose targeted skills.

Three leveled, reproducible activity sheets are provided for each core skill. Levels are indicated by the number of small circles at the bottom of each activity sheet:

- Basic

- Intermediate

- Challenging

How to Use This Book

- Tiered assignments are one way to provide tasks at varying levels. For each chosen skill, teachers should target a level based on the readiness of an individual student. For example, assign basic tasks to struggling learners and assign challenging tasks to advanced learners. With this strategy, students focus on the same skill while working at their individual ability levels.

- Another approach is to have each student progress through the levels as he gains essential understanding or proficiency of each featured skill. This frequent, focused practice will help maximize student retention.

Other Suggestions

- As students progress through each level, document their progress on a generic class list. This provides additional documentation regarding student progress for administrators and parents.

- Use the readiness levels to form flexible groups for targeted instruction.

- Utilize the basic level skill sheets for student remediation.

- Review previously taught core skills with targeted learning activities.

- Form peer tutoring partnerships using students from basic/intermediate and intermediate/challenging level groups.

Name: _____   Date: _____

Place Value

Five-digit numbers have five parts: the ten thousands place, the thousands place, the hundreds place, the tens place, and the ones place.

56,379 =

Ten Thousands	Thousands	Hundreds	Tens	Ones
5	6	3	7	9

fifty-six thousand three hundred seventy-nine

Use the code below to color the butterfly.

3 thousands = blue	5 hundreds = red	I ten = green
3 hundreds = orange	2 ten thousands = yellow	

1.

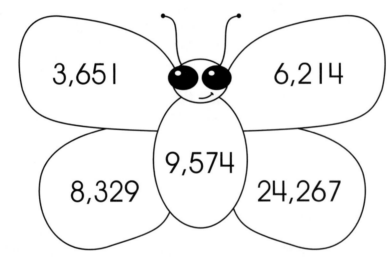

Write the matching number or number words for each problem.

2. 42,163 = _____

    _____

3. thirty-one thousand four hundred twenty-one = _____

4. sixty-one thousand five hundred sixty-four = _____

5. 97,358 = _____

    _____

Name: _____   Date: _____

Place Value

Six-digit numbers have six parts: the hundred thousands place, the ten thousands place, the thousands place, the hundreds place, the tens place, and the ones place.

182,457 =

Hundred Thousands	Ten Thousands	Thousands	Hundreds	Tens	Ones
1	8	2	4	5	7

one hundred eighty-two thousand four hundred fifty-seven

Write the digits in the correct place value.

1. 523,186

hundred thousands _____

ten thousands _____

thousands _____

hundreds _____

tens _____

ones _____

2. 89,207

hundred thousands _____

ten thousands _____

thousands _____

hundreds _____

tens _____

ones _____

3. 834,651

hundred thousands _____

ten thousands _____

thousands _____

hundreds _____

tens _____

ones _____

Fill in the blanks.

4. 932,769   The three is in the _____ place.

5. 587,643   The seven is in the _____ place.

6. 118,209   The zero is in the _____ place.

7. 531,670   The five is in the _____ place.

8. 981,234   The two is in the _____ place.

9. 205,689   The nine is in the _____ place.

10. 482,775   The eight is in the _____ place.

Name: _____ Date: _____

Place Value

Review the example below for place values up to the hundred billions.

Billions			Millions			Thousands			Ones		
Hundred Billions	Ten Billions	Billions	Hundred Millions	Ten Millions	Millions	Hundred Thousands	Ten Thousands	Thousands	Hundreds	Tens	Ones
8	4	2	1	9	6	3	4	5	2	0	1

842,196,345,201 = eight hundred forty-two billion one hundred ninety-six million three hundred forty-five thousand two hundred one

Write the value of each underlined digit.

1. 746,196

2. 8,946,243,000

3. 852,146,306

4. 965,409

5. 3,428,998

6. 78,456

7. 3,543,192

8. 406,294

9. 706,421,599

10. 2,416,349,187

11. 474,891,176

12. 845,317,764,249

Write each number in word form.

13. 3,421,800,000 _____

_____

_____

14. 45,982,406,399 _____

_____

_____

_____

Rounding Numbers

When rounding to the nearest hundred, follow these steps:

1. Look at the tens place.
2. If the digit is 0, 1, 2, 3, or 4, round down.
3. If the digit is 5, 6, 7, 8, or 9, round up.

Examples: 744 rounds down to 700; 782 rounds up to 800

Round the amount in each treasure chest to the nearest hundred.

1.
$692
$ _____

2.
$140
$ _____

3.
$569
$ _____

4.
$303
$ _____

5.
$684
$ _____

6.
$851
$ _____

7.
$712
$ _____

8.
$476
$ _____

9.
$925
$ _____

Name: _____ Date: _____

Rounding Numbers

When rounding to the nearest thousand, follow these steps:
1. Look at the hundreds place.
2. If the digit is 0, 1, 2, 3, or 4, round down.
3. If the digit is 5, 6, 7, 8, or 9, round up.
Examples: 4,399 rounds down to 4,000; 4,683 rounds up to 5,000

Round to the nearest ten.

1. 72 _____   2. 55 _____   3. 14 _____   4. 62 _____

5. 83 _____   6. 17 _____   7. 49 _____   8. 29 _____

Round to the nearest hundred.

9. 284 _____   10. 924 _____   11. 561 _____   12. 354 _____

13. 752 _____   14. 728 _____   15. 689 _____   16. 192 _____

Round to the nearest thousand.

17. 1,432 _____   18. 2,418 _____   19. 1,242 _____

20. 4,299 _____   21. 6,419 _____   22. 7,546 _____

23. 9,721 _____   24. 4,142 _____   25. 5,948 _____

Name: _____ Date: _____

Rounding Numbers

When rounding to the nearest million, follow these steps:
1. Look at the hundred thousands place.
2. If the digit is 0, 1, 2, 3, or 4, round down.
3. If the digit is 5, 6, 7, 8, or 9, round up.

Examples: 5,265,057 rounds down to 5,000,000; 5,824,674 rounds up to 6,000,000

Round to the nearest thousand.

1. 7,539	2. 8,762	3. 1,252	4. 3,493	5. 6,504
6. 8,433	7. 5,421	8. 9,741	9. 5,921	10. 7,438

Round to the nearest ten thousand.

11. 64,296	12. 54,989	13. 76,489	14. 38,496	15. 25,492
16. 23,986	17. 42,776	18. 84,980	19. 55,250	20. 68,022

Round to the nearest million.

21. 1,905,276	22. 3,480,972	23. 6,914,370
24. 5,479,140	25. 6,482,612	26. 1,749,057

Name: _____ Date: _____

Comparing Numbers

When comparing numbers, you are deciding which number is the greatest and which number is the least. The symbol > means **greater than** and the symbol < means **less than**. Follow these steps to compare numbers:

1. Look at the number of digits in both numbers. Are they the same? If not, the number with the most digits is greater.
2. If the number of digits is the same, begin with the first digit on the left. Which number has a larger digit? That is the greater number.
3. If the digits are the same, move to the next place value and find the larger digit.

671 $<$ 2,318

2,318 has more digits, so it is the greater number.

564 $>$ 372

The first digit in 564 (5) is greater, so it is the greater number.

671 $>$ 619

The number of digits is the same. The first digits are the same. The second digit in 671 (7) is greater, so it is the greater number.

Write > or < to compare each pair of numbers.

1. 317 ◯ 1,198

2. 298 ◯ 300

3. 982 ◯ 918

4. 761 ◯ 760

5. 29 ◯ 30

6. 4,395 ◯ 4,217

7. 176 ◯ 134

8. 512 ◯ 514

9. 803 ◯ 850

10. 6,330 ◯ 3,630

Step Up to Math · Intermediate · CD-104260 · © Carson-Dellosa

Name: _____   Date: _____

Comparing Numbers

The greater than (>) and less than (<) symbols always open toward the number of greater value and point to the number of lesser value. Numbers of equal value use the equal sign (=). To compare numbers, follow these steps:

1. Look at the number of digits in both numbers. Are they the same? If not, the number with the most digits is greater.
2. If the number of digits is the same, begin with the first digit on the left. Which number has a larger digit? That is the greater number.
3. If the digits are the same, move to the next place value and find the larger digit.

Examples: 6,443 > 5,308; 3,440 < 3,592; 21,204 = 21,204

Write >, <, or = to compare each pair of numbers.

1.   10,561 ◯ 10,660   2.   4,128 ◯ 2,199   3.   2,145 ◯ 8,415

4.   1,834 ◯ 1,843   5.   21,542 ◯ 21,249   6.   4,809 ◯ 4,809

7.   6,424 ◯ 6,414   8.   1,215 ◯ 5,187   9.   9,214 ◯ 4,482

10.   351 ◯ 350   11.   51,215 ◯ 51,215   12.   3,814 ◯ 4,285

13.   921 ◯ 9,219   14.   319,114 ◯ 312,546   15.   2,312 ◯ 5,645

16.   221,048 ◯ 221,648   17.   15,198 ◯ 41,426   18.   8,249 ◯ 511

Comparing Numbers

The greater than (>) and less than (<) symbols always open toward the number of greater value and point to the number of lesser value. Numbers of equal value use the equal sign (=).

To order numbers from least to greatest, compare all of the numbers. Place the number with the lowest value first and then arrange the remaining numbers in order.

Example: 249,005   198,724   229,459 is ordered 198,724   229,459   249,005

Write >, <, or = to compare each pair of numbers.

1. 25,064 ◯ 27,590   2. 56,000 ◯ 56,000   3. 2,641 ◯ 3,461

4. 17,048 ◯ 15,084   5. 22,728 ◯ 22,782   6. 55,491 ◯ 55,941

7. 8,463 ◯ 6,891   8. 85,485 ◯ 89,849   9. 74,912 ◯ 43,819

10. 83,214 ◯ 83,214   11. 54,295 ◯ 82,918   12. 924,146 ◯ 948,962

Order each set of numbers from least to greatest.

13. 1,408,241   9,426,597   1,400,892

_____

14. 342,192   328,191   340,384

_____

15. 68,297   405,495   929,058   65,382

_____

Adding with Regrouping

Sometimes when adding, the sum of a column is 10 or higher. When this happens, regroup to the next place value column. To regroup, follow these steps:

1. Add the ones. Regroup the 10 ones as 1 ten.

2. Add the tens. Regroup to the hundreds column if necessary.

3. Add the hundreds.

$$
\begin{array}{r} {}^{1}\\ 173 \\ + 428 \\ \hline 1 \end{array}
\qquad
\begin{array}{r} {}^{1\ 1}\\ 173 \\ + 428 \\ \hline 01 \end{array}
\qquad
\begin{array}{r} {}^{1\ 1}\\ 173 \\ + 428 \\ \hline 601 \end{array}
$$

Add.

1. $\begin{array}{r} 57 \\ + 28 \\ \hline \end{array}$ 2. $\begin{array}{r} 36 \\ + 46 \\ \hline \end{array}$ 3. $\begin{array}{r} 73 \\ + 17 \\ \hline \end{array}$ 4. $\begin{array}{r} 39 \\ + 29 \\ \hline \end{array}$ 5. $\begin{array}{r} 14 \\ + 17 \\ \hline \end{array}$

6. $\begin{array}{r} 35 \\ + 15 \\ \hline \end{array}$ 7. $\begin{array}{r} 364 \\ + 271 \\ \hline \end{array}$ 8. $\begin{array}{r} 591 \\ + 186 \\ \hline \end{array}$ 9. $\begin{array}{r} 869 \\ + 80 \\ \hline \end{array}$ 10. $\begin{array}{r} 453 \\ + 364 \\ \hline \end{array}$

11. $\begin{array}{r} 272 \\ + 96 \\ \hline \end{array}$ 12. $\begin{array}{r} 291 \\ + 285 \\ \hline \end{array}$ 13. $\begin{array}{r} 106 \\ + 106 \\ \hline \end{array}$ 14. $\begin{array}{r} 319 \\ + 78 \\ \hline \end{array}$ 15. $\begin{array}{r} 346 \\ + 628 \\ \hline \end{array}$

Adding with Regrouping

Sometimes when adding, the sum of a column is 10 or higher. When this happens, regroup to the next column. To regroup, follow these steps:

1. Add the ones. Regroup if necessary.

$$\begin{array}{r} {}^{1} \\ 3{,}465 \\ +\ 2{,}597 \\ \hline 2 \end{array}$$

2. Add the tens. Regroup if necessary.

$$\begin{array}{r} {}^{1\,1} \\ 3{,}465 \\ +\ 2{,}597 \\ \hline 62 \end{array}$$

3. Add the hundreds. Regroup if necessary.

$$\begin{array}{r} {}^{1\,1\,1} \\ 3{,}465 \\ +\ 2{,}597 \\ \hline 062 \end{array}$$

4. Add the thousands. Regroup if necessary.

$$\begin{array}{r} {}^{1\,1\,1} \\ 3{,}465 \\ +\ 2{,}597 \\ \hline 6{,}062 \end{array}$$

Add.

1. 3,421
    + 9,947

2. 6,429
    + 1,843

3. 9,249
    + 2,137

4. 5,429
    + 3,870

5. 6,484
    + 2,929

6. 7,642
    + 1,859

7. 7,298
    + 2,846

8. 5,421
    + 8,298

9. 6,489
    + 2,576

10. 3,465
    + 2,987

11. 5,642
    + 2,987

12. 3,841
    + 2,839

13. 34,215
    + 25,398

14. 19,648
    + 81,349

15. 72,817
    + 39,798

16. 67,918
    + 38,217

Name: _____ Date: _____

Adding with Regrouping

Sometimes when adding, the sum of a column is 10 or higher. When this happens, regroup to the next column. To regroup, follow these steps:

1. Add the ones. Regroup if necessary.

$$\begin{array}{r} \overset{1}{14{,}836} \\ + 11{,}987 \\ \hline 3 \end{array}$$

2. Add the tens. Regroup if necessary

$$\begin{array}{r} \overset{1\,1}{14{,}836} \\ + 11{,}987 \\ \hline 23 \end{array}$$

3. Add the hundreds. Regroup if necessary.

$$\begin{array}{r} \overset{1\,1\,1}{14{,}836} \\ + 11{,}987 \\ \hline 823 \end{array}$$

4. Add the thousands. Regroup if necessary.

$$\begin{array}{r} \overset{1\,1\,1}{14{,}836} \\ + 11{,}987 \\ \hline 6{,}823 \end{array}$$

5. Add the ten thousands. Regroup if necessary.

$$\begin{array}{r} \overset{1\,1\,1}{14{,}836} \\ + 11{,}987 \\ \hline 26{,}823 \end{array}$$

Add.

1.
$$\begin{array}{r} 7{,}432 \\ + 1{,}298 \\ \hline \end{array}$$

2.
$$\begin{array}{r} 5{,}068 \\ + 2{,}753 \\ \hline \end{array}$$

3.
$$\begin{array}{r} 8{,}430 \\ + 2{,}193 \\ \hline \end{array}$$

4.
$$\begin{array}{r} 2{,}573 \\ + 1{,}842 \\ \hline \end{array}$$

5.
$$\begin{array}{r} 64{,}413 \\ + \quad 389 \\ \hline \end{array}$$

6.
$$\begin{array}{r} 4{,}568 \\ + \quad 978 \\ \hline \end{array}$$

7.
$$\begin{array}{r} 32{,}146 \\ + 13{,}927 \\ \hline \end{array}$$

8.
$$\begin{array}{r} 41{,}387 \\ + 2{,}176 \\ \hline \end{array}$$

9.
$$\begin{array}{r} 56{,}143 \\ + \quad 2{,}478 \\ \hline \end{array}$$

10.
$$\begin{array}{r} 72{,}615 \\ + 23{,}827 \\ \hline \end{array}$$

11.
$$\begin{array}{r} 42{,}516 \\ + 19{,}827 \\ \hline \end{array}$$

12.
$$\begin{array}{r} 56{,}247 \\ + 17{,}085 \\ \hline \end{array}$$

13.
$$\begin{array}{r} 62{,}148 \\ + 19{,}382 \\ \hline \end{array}$$

14.
$$\begin{array}{r} 92{,}416 \\ + 13{,}592 \\ \hline \end{array}$$

15.
$$\begin{array}{r} 25{,}146 \\ + 26{,}328 \\ \hline \end{array}$$

16.
$$\begin{array}{r} 42{,}158 \\ + 51{,}319 \\ \hline \end{array}$$

Subtracting with Regrouping

Sometimes when subtracting, it is necessary to regroup from a higher place value column to a lower place value column. To regroup more than once, follow these steps:

1. Try to subtract the ones. Regroup from the tens if necessary.

$$\begin{array}{r} {\scriptstyle 4\ 13} \\ 6\,5\!\!\!/\,3\!\!\!/ \\ -\ 2\ 8\ 4 \\ \hline 9 \end{array}$$

2. Try to subtract the tens. Regroup from the hundreds if necessary.

$$\begin{array}{r} {\scriptstyle 14} \\ {\scriptstyle 5\ \cancel{6}\,13} \\ \cancel{6}\,\cancel{5}\,\cancel{3} \\ -\ 2\ 8\ 4 \\ \hline 6\ 9 \end{array}$$

3. Subtract the hundreds.

$$\begin{array}{r} {\scriptstyle 14} \\ {\scriptstyle 5\ \cancel{6}\,13} \\ \cancel{6}\,\cancel{5}\,\cancel{3} \\ -\ 2\ 8\ 4 \\ \hline 3\ 6\ 9 \end{array}$$

Subtract.

1. $\begin{array}{r}912\\-\ 656\\\hline\end{array}$	2. $\begin{array}{r}851\\-\ 184\\\hline\end{array}$	3. $\begin{array}{r}463\\-\ 248\\\hline\end{array}$	4. $\begin{array}{r}367\\-\ 193\\\hline\end{array}$	5. $\begin{array}{r}624\\-\ 218\\\hline\end{array}$
6. $\begin{array}{r}151\\-\ 124\\\hline\end{array}$	7. $\begin{array}{r}931\\-\ 736\\\hline\end{array}$	8. $\begin{array}{r}452\\-\ 198\\\hline\end{array}$	9. $\begin{array}{r}662\\-\ 279\\\hline\end{array}$	10. $\begin{array}{r}528\\-\ 139\\\hline\end{array}$
11. $\begin{array}{r}851\\-\ 485\\\hline\end{array}$	12. $\begin{array}{r}746\\-\ 247\\\hline\end{array}$	13. $\begin{array}{r}813\\-\ 461\\\hline\end{array}$	14. $\begin{array}{r}963\\-\ 728\\\hline\end{array}$	15. $\begin{array}{r}385\\-\ 191\\\hline\end{array}$

Name: _____   Date: _____

Subtracting with Regrouping

Sometimes when subtracting, it is necessary to regroup from a higher place value column to a lower place value column. To regroup more than once, follow these steps:

1. Try to subtract the ones. Regroup from the tens if necessary.

$$\begin{array}{r} {\scriptstyle 3\ 13} \\ 3,1\cancel{4}\cancel{3} \\ -\ 1,825 \\ \hline 8 \end{array}$$

2. Try to subtract the tens. Regroup from the hundreds if necessary.

$$\begin{array}{r} {\scriptstyle 3\ 13} \\ 3,1\cancel{4}\cancel{3} \\ -\ 1,825 \\ \hline 18 \end{array}$$

3. Try to subtract the hundreds. Regroup from the thousands if necessary.

$$\begin{array}{r} {\scriptstyle 2\ 11\ 3\ 13} \\ \cancel{3},\cancel{1}\cancel{4}\cancel{3} \\ -\ 1,825 \\ \hline 318 \end{array}$$

4. Subtract the thousands.

$$\begin{array}{r} {\scriptstyle 2\ 11\ 3\ 13} \\ \cancel{3},\cancel{1}\cancel{4}\cancel{3} \\ -\ 1,825 \\ \hline 1,318 \end{array}$$

Subtract.

1. 642 − 384

2. 549 − 293

3. 754 − 628

4. 592 − 328

5. 462 − 285

6. 744 − 256

7. 2,143 − 1,385

8. 7,469 − 3,873

9. 4,685 − 298

10. 6,435 − 4,972

11. 9,846 − 928

12. 3,764 − 1,878

13. 5,648 − 3,959

14. 4,657 − 2,879

15. 8,408 − 6,519

16. 7,645 − 3,789

Subtracting with Regrouping

Sometimes when subtracting, it is necessary to regroup from a higher place value column to a lower place value column. To regroup more than once, follow these steps:

1. Try to subtract the ones. Regroup if necessary.	2. Try to subtract the tens. Regroup if necessary.	3. Try to subtract the hundreds. Regroup if necessary.	4. Try to subtract the thousands. Regroup if necessary.	5. Subtract the ten thousands.
3 15 62,1⁄4⁄5⁄ −28,356 ───── 9	0 13 15 62,⁄1⁄4⁄5⁄ −28,356 ───── 89	1 10 13 15 62,⁄1⁄4⁄5⁄ −28,356 ───── 789	5 11 10 13 15 ⁄6⁄2,⁄1⁄4⁄5⁄ −28,356 ───── 3,789	5 11 10 13 15 ⁄6⁄2,⁄1⁄4⁄5⁄ −28,356 ───── 33,789

Subtract.

1.	23,153 − 11,245	2.	44,528 − 31,392	3.	67,643 − 42,818	4.	35,420 − 11,287
5.	87,645 − 81,829	6.	43,843 − 21,927	7.	36,412 − 24,829	8.	56,218 − 28,303
9.	89,516 − 28,138	10.	36,142 − 18,195	11.	58,418 − 29,312	12.	76,413 − 48,321
13.	49,218 − 18,309	14.	92,142 − 68,037	15.	77,642 − 45,855	16.	29,280 − 13,417

Subtracting with Zeros

To subtract from a 0, follow these steps:

1. Try to subtract the ones. Regroup 1 ten as 10 ones.

$$\begin{array}{r} {\scriptstyle 3\,10} \\ \cancel{40} \\ -\ 28 \\ \hline 2 \end{array}$$

2. Subtract the tens.

$$\begin{array}{r} {\scriptstyle 3\,10} \\ \cancel{40} \\ -\ 28 \\ \hline 12 \end{array}$$

Subtract.

1. $\begin{array}{r}30\\-17\\\hline\end{array}$	2. $\begin{array}{r}70\\-49\\\hline\end{array}$	3. $\begin{array}{r}80\\-59\\\hline\end{array}$	4. $\begin{array}{r}70\\-46\\\hline\end{array}$
5. $\begin{array}{r}40\\-32\\\hline\end{array}$	6. $\begin{array}{r}50\\-34\\\hline\end{array}$	7. $\begin{array}{r}40\\-29\\\hline\end{array}$	8. $\begin{array}{r}60\\-48\\\hline\end{array}$
9. $\begin{array}{r}60\\-18\\\hline\end{array}$	10. $\begin{array}{r}50\\-38\\\hline\end{array}$	11. $\begin{array}{r}20\\-18\\\hline\end{array}$	12. $\begin{array}{r}40\\-25\\\hline\end{array}$
13. $\begin{array}{r}80\\-47\\\hline\end{array}$	14. $\begin{array}{r}70\\-45\\\hline\end{array}$	15. $\begin{array}{r}40\\-15\\\hline\end{array}$	16. $\begin{array}{r}80\\-39\\\hline\end{array}$
17. $\begin{array}{r}50\\-17\\\hline\end{array}$	18. $\begin{array}{r}60\\-12\\\hline\end{array}$	19. $\begin{array}{r}70\\-34\\\hline\end{array}$	20. $\begin{array}{r}40\\-28\\\hline\end{array}$

Name: _____   Date: _____

Subtracting with Zeros

When regrouping across zeros, regroup from the first place value column that does not have a zero. Regroup each 0 by changing it to a 10. Then, regroup from each 10 by changing it to a 9. To subtract from a 0, follow these steps:

1. Try to subtract the ones. Regroup each 0 by changing it to a 10. Regroup from each 10 by changing it to a 9.

```
    9 9
  6 10 10 12
   7,0 0 2
 - 1,879
       3
```

2. Try to subtract the tens. Regroup if necessary.

```
    9 9
  6 10 10 12
   7,0 0 2
 - 1,879
      23
```

3. Try to subtract the hundreds. Regroup if necessary.

```
    9 9
  6 10 10 12
   7,0 0 2
 - 1,879
     123
```

4. Subtract the thousands.

```
    9 9
  6 10 10 12
   7,0 0 2
 - 1,879
   5,123
```

Subtract.

1. 508 − 142

2. 640 − 239

3. 250 − 128

4. 700 − 124

5. 700 − 527

6. 808 − 564

7. 3,006 − 1,242

8. 6,240 − 4,193

9. 9,040 − 2,318

10. 7,048 − 6,529

11. 3,000 − 147

12. 9,048 − 329

13. 6,408 − 2,299

14. 5,000 − 2,084

15. 8,405 − 521

16. 4,205 − 812

Subtracting with Zeros

When regrouping across zeros, regroup from the first place value column that does not have a zero. Regroup each 0 by changing it to a 10. Then, regroup from each 10 by changing it to a 9. To subtract from a 0, follow these steps:

1. Try to subtract the ones. Regroup each 0 by changing it to a 10. Regroup from each 10 by changing it to a 9.

$$\begin{array}{r} 7{,}002 \\ -\ 1{,}879 \\ \hline 3 \end{array}$$

2. Try to subtract the tens. Regroup if necessary.

$$\begin{array}{r} 7{,}002 \\ -\ 1{,}879 \\ \hline 23 \end{array}$$

3. Try to subtract the hundreds. Regroup if necessary.

$$\begin{array}{r} 7{,}002 \\ -\ 1{,}879 \\ \hline 123 \end{array}$$

4. Subtract the thousands.

$$\begin{array}{r} 7{,}002 \\ -\ 1{,}879 \\ \hline 5{,}123 \end{array}$$

Subtract.

1.
$$\begin{array}{r} 3{,}160 \\ -\ 2{,}268 \\ \hline \end{array}$$

2.
$$\begin{array}{r} 26{,}700 \\ -\ 23{,}727 \\ \hline \end{array}$$

3.
$$\begin{array}{r} 103{,}400 \\ -\ 95{,}128 \\ \hline \end{array}$$

4.
$$\begin{array}{r} 85{,}600 \\ -\ 83{,}248 \\ \hline \end{array}$$

5.
$$\begin{array}{r} 110{,}800 \\ -\ 106{,}547 \\ \hline \end{array}$$

6.
$$\begin{array}{r} 40{,}200 \\ -\ 38{,}146 \\ \hline \end{array}$$

7.
$$\begin{array}{r} 63{,}301 \\ -\ 62{,}342 \\ \hline \end{array}$$

8.
$$\begin{array}{r} 186{,}520 \\ -\ 185{,}545 \\ \hline \end{array}$$

9.
$$\begin{array}{r} 98{,}750 \\ -\ 9{,}955 \\ \hline \end{array}$$

10.
$$\begin{array}{r} 12{,}700 \\ -\ 8{,}568 \\ \hline \end{array}$$

11.
$$\begin{array}{r} 301{,}040 \\ -\ 203{,}829 \\ \hline \end{array}$$

12.
$$\begin{array}{r} 76{,}090 \\ -\ 63{,}867 \\ \hline \end{array}$$

13.
$$\begin{array}{r} 69{,}002 \\ -\ 53{,}846 \\ \hline \end{array}$$

14.
$$\begin{array}{r} 249{,}300 \\ -\ 237{,}208 \\ \hline \end{array}$$

15.
$$\begin{array}{r} 46{,}000 \\ -\ 14{,}235 \\ \hline \end{array}$$

16.
$$\begin{array}{r} 605{,}008 \\ -\ 123{,}124 \\ \hline \end{array}$$

Basic Multiplication

When multiplying by 10, write a zero in the ones place. Then, multiply by 1.

Example: Write a zero in   Multiply by 1.
            the ones place.

```
      27                    27
    x 10                  x 10
    -----                 -----
       0                   270
```

Multiply.

```
1.    85        2.    36        3.    66        4.    38        5.    17
    x 10            x 10            x 10            x 10            x 10
    -----           -----           -----           -----           -----


6.    49        7.    88        8.    14        9.    71       10.    82
    x 10            x 10            x 10            x 10            x 10
    -----           -----           -----           -----           -----


11.   65       12.    28       13.    93       14.    33       15.    86
    x 10            x 10            x 10            x 10            x 10
    -----           -----           -----           -----           -----


16.   22       17.    46       18.    70       19.    87       20.    64
    x 10            x 10            x 10            x 10            x 10
    -----           -----           -----           -----           -----
```

Basic Multiplication

When multiplying by 100, write a zero in the ones place and the tens place. Then, multiply by 1.

Example: Write a zero in the ones   Multiply by 1.
            place and the tens place.

```
        625                              625
      x 100                            x 100
      ------                           -------
         00                            62,500
```

Multiply.

1.   642   2.   323   3.   496   4.   165
    x 100   x 100   x 100   x 100

5.   649   6.   874   7.   940   8.   528
    x 100   x 100   x 100   x 100

9.   805   10.   764   11.   214   12.   295
    x 100   x 100   x 100   x 100

13.   830   14.   384   15.   903   16.   472
    x 100   x 100   x 100   x 100

17.   381   18.   168   19.   247   20.   687
    x 100   x 100   x 100   x 100

Name: _____ Date: _____

Basic Multiplication

When multiplying by 1,000, write a zero in the ones place, the tens place, and the hundreds place. Then, multiply by 1.

Example: Write a zero in the ones place, the tens place, and the hundreds place.

```
   618
x 1,000
-------
   000
```

Multiply by 1.

```
   618
x 1,000
-------
 618,000
```

Multiply.

1. 165
x 1,000

2. 982
x 1,000

3. 756
x 1,000

4. 240
x 1,000

5. 452
x 1,000

6. 598
x 1,000

7. 265
x 1,000

8. 422
x 1,000

9. 326
x 1,000

10. 584
x 1,000

11. 649
x 1,000

12. 467
x 1,000

13. 687
x 1,000

14. 806
x 1,000

15. 256
x 1,000

16. 590
x 1,000

17. 238
x 1,000

18. 198
x 1,000

19. 201
x 1,000

20. 485
x 1,000

Step Up to Math · Intermediate · CD-104260 · © Carson-Dellosa

Name: _____ Date: _____

Multiplying by One-Digit Numbers

To multiply by a one-digit number, follow these steps:

1. Multiply the ones by the one-digit number. Regroup if necessary.

$$\begin{array}{r} \overset{1}{3}2 \\ \times\ 6 \\ \hline 2 \end{array}$$

2. Multiply the tens by the one-digit number. Add the regrouped amount.

$$\begin{array}{r} \overset{1}{3}2 \\ \times\ 6 \\ \hline 192 \end{array}$$

Multiply.

1. $\begin{array}{r} 94 \\ \times\ 3 \\ \hline \end{array}$
2. $\begin{array}{r} 24 \\ \times\ 7 \\ \hline \end{array}$
3. $\begin{array}{r} 36 \\ \times\ 9 \\ \hline \end{array}$
4. $\begin{array}{r} 37 \\ \times\ 5 \\ \hline \end{array}$
5. $\begin{array}{r} 59 \\ \times\ 8 \\ \hline \end{array}$

6. $\begin{array}{r} 32 \\ \times\ 2 \\ \hline \end{array}$
7. $\begin{array}{r} 28 \\ \times\ 3 \\ \hline \end{array}$
8. $\begin{array}{r} 72 \\ \times\ 7 \\ \hline \end{array}$
9. $\begin{array}{r} 43 \\ \times\ 5 \\ \hline \end{array}$
10. $\begin{array}{r} 24 \\ \times\ 6 \\ \hline \end{array}$

11. $\begin{array}{r} 34 \\ \times\ 6 \\ \hline \end{array}$
12. $\begin{array}{r} 94 \\ \times\ 3 \\ \hline \end{array}$
13. $\begin{array}{r} 86 \\ \times\ 7 \\ \hline \end{array}$
14. $\begin{array}{r} 58 \\ \times\ 5 \\ \hline \end{array}$
15. $\begin{array}{r} 47 \\ \times\ 8 \\ \hline \end{array}$

16. $\begin{array}{r} 43 \\ \times\ 2 \\ \hline \end{array}$
17. $\begin{array}{r} 31 \\ \times\ 6 \\ \hline \end{array}$
18. $\begin{array}{r} 24 \\ \times\ 8 \\ \hline \end{array}$
19. $\begin{array}{r} 32 \\ \times\ 4 \\ \hline \end{array}$
20. $\begin{array}{r} 21 \\ \times\ 7 \\ \hline \end{array}$

Name: _____   Date: _____

Multiplying by One-Digit Numbers

To multiply by a one-digit number, follow these steps:

1. Multiply the ones by the one-digit number. Regroup if necessary.

2. Multiply the tens by the one-digit number. Add the regrouped amount. Regroup if necessary.

3. Multiply the hundreds by the one-digit number. Add the regrouped amount.

$$
\begin{array}{r}
{\scriptstyle 2} \\
279 \\
\times \quad 3 \\
\hline
7
\end{array}
\qquad
\begin{array}{r}
{\scriptstyle 2\,2} \\
279 \\
\times \quad 3 \\
\hline
37
\end{array}
\qquad
\begin{array}{r}
{\scriptstyle 2\,2} \\
279 \\
\times \quad 3 \\
\hline
837
\end{array}
$$

Multiply.

1. $\begin{array}{r} 214 \\ \times \quad 3 \\ \hline \end{array}$ 2. $\begin{array}{r} 284 \\ \times \quad 2 \\ \hline \end{array}$ 3. $\begin{array}{r} 510 \\ \times \quad 5 \\ \hline \end{array}$ 4. $\begin{array}{r} 243 \\ \times \quad 4 \\ \hline \end{array}$ 5. $\begin{array}{r} 131 \\ \times \quad 8 \\ \hline \end{array}$

6. $\begin{array}{r} 123 \\ \times \quad 6 \\ \hline \end{array}$ 7. $\begin{array}{r} 514 \\ \times \quad 4 \\ \hline \end{array}$ 8. $\begin{array}{r} 213 \\ \times \quad 7 \\ \hline \end{array}$ 9. $\begin{array}{r} 412 \\ \times \quad 9 \\ \hline \end{array}$ 10. $\begin{array}{r} 842 \\ \times \quad 3 \\ \hline \end{array}$

11. $\begin{array}{r} 354 \\ \times \quad 5 \\ \hline \end{array}$ 12. $\begin{array}{r} 126 \\ \times \quad 8 \\ \hline \end{array}$ 13. $\begin{array}{r} 408 \\ \times \quad 6 \\ \hline \end{array}$ 14. $\begin{array}{r} 237 \\ \times \quad 3 \\ \hline \end{array}$ 15. $\begin{array}{r} 543 \\ \times \quad 4 \\ \hline \end{array}$

16. $\begin{array}{r} 985 \\ \times \quad 2 \\ \hline \end{array}$ 17. $\begin{array}{r} 168 \\ \times \quad 5 \\ \hline \end{array}$ 18. $\begin{array}{r} 863 \\ \times \quad 9 \\ \hline \end{array}$ 19. $\begin{array}{r} 379 \\ \times \quad 6 \\ \hline \end{array}$ 20. $\begin{array}{r} 974 \\ \times \quad 7 \\ \hline \end{array}$

Multiplying by One-Digit Numbers

To multiply by a one-digit number, follow these steps:

1. Multiply the ones by the one-digit number. Regroup if necessary.

$$\begin{array}{r} {}^{4} \\ 4{,}238 \\ \times \quad 6 \\ \hline 8 \end{array}$$

2. Multiply the tens by the one-digit number. Add the regrouped amount. Regroup if necessary.

$$\begin{array}{r} {}^{2\,4} \\ 4{,}238 \\ \times \quad 6 \\ \hline 28 \end{array}$$

3. Multiply the hundreds by the one-digit number. Add the regrouped amount. Regroup if necessary.

$$\begin{array}{r} {}^{1\,2\,4} \\ 4{,}238 \\ \times \quad 6 \\ \hline 428 \end{array}$$

4. Multiply the thousands by the one-digit number. Add the regrouped amount.

$$\begin{array}{r} {}^{1\,2\,4} \\ 4{,}238 \\ \times \quad 6 \\ \hline 25{,}428 \end{array}$$

Multiply.

1. $\begin{array}{r} 3{,}123 \\ \times \quad 3 \\ \hline \end{array}$

2. $\begin{array}{r} 4{,}243 \\ \times \quad 2 \\ \hline \end{array}$

3. $\begin{array}{r} 4{,}321 \\ \times \quad 6 \\ \hline \end{array}$

4. $\begin{array}{r} 1{,}228 \\ \times \quad 4 \\ \hline \end{array}$

5. $\begin{array}{r} 2{,}752 \\ \times \quad 4 \\ \hline \end{array}$

6. $\begin{array}{r} 4{,}523 \\ \times \quad 5 \\ \hline \end{array}$

7. $\begin{array}{r} 8{,}463 \\ \times \quad 2 \\ \hline \end{array}$

8. $\begin{array}{r} 8{,}427 \\ \times \quad 3 \\ \hline \end{array}$

9. $\begin{array}{r} 5{,}139 \\ \times \quad 6 \\ \hline \end{array}$

10. $\begin{array}{r} 4{,}687 \\ \times \quad 3 \\ \hline \end{array}$

11. $\begin{array}{r} 2{,}341 \\ \times \quad 8 \\ \hline \end{array}$

12. $\begin{array}{r} 4{,}613 \\ \times \quad 7 \\ \hline \end{array}$

13. $\begin{array}{r} 2{,}843 \\ \times \quad 3 \\ \hline \end{array}$

14. $\begin{array}{r} 4{,}456 \\ \times \quad 5 \\ \hline \end{array}$

15. $\begin{array}{r} 1{,}621 \\ \times \quad 6 \\ \hline \end{array}$

16. $\begin{array}{r} 2{,}815 \\ \times \quad 8 \\ \hline \end{array}$

Name: _____   Date: _____

Multiplying by Two-Digit Numbers

To multiply by a two-digit number, follow these steps:

1. Multiply the top number by the ones digit in the second number. Regroup if necessary.

2. Write a zero in the ones column.

3. Multiply the top number by the tens digit in the second number. Regroup if necessary.

4. Add. Regroup if necessary.

```
      28
    x 60
    ─────
      00
```

```
      28
    x 60
    ─────
      00
       0
```

```
       4
      28
    x 60
    ─────
      00
  + 1,680
```

```
       4
      28
    x 60
    ─────
      00
  + 1,680
  ───────
    1,680
```

Multiply.

1. $\begin{array}{r} 21 \\ \times\ 30 \\ \hline \end{array}$	2. $\begin{array}{r} 22 \\ \times\ 40 \\ \hline \end{array}$	3. $\begin{array}{r} 27 \\ \times\ 30 \\ \hline \end{array}$	4. $\begin{array}{r} 57 \\ \times\ 40 \\ \hline \end{array}$	5. $\begin{array}{r} 23 \\ \times\ 50 \\ \hline \end{array}$
6. $\begin{array}{r} 23 \\ \times\ 40 \\ \hline \end{array}$	7. $\begin{array}{r} 25 \\ \times\ 60 \\ \hline \end{array}$	8. $\begin{array}{r} 28 \\ \times\ 40 \\ \hline \end{array}$	9. $\begin{array}{r} 28 \\ \times\ 20 \\ \hline \end{array}$	10. $\begin{array}{r} 69 \\ \times\ 30 \\ \hline \end{array}$
11. $\begin{array}{r} 36 \\ \times\ 70 \\ \hline \end{array}$	12. $\begin{array}{r} 13 \\ \times\ 80 \\ \hline \end{array}$	13. $\begin{array}{r} 28 \\ \times\ 40 \\ \hline \end{array}$	14. $\begin{array}{r} 89 \\ \times\ 40 \\ \hline \end{array}$	15. $\begin{array}{r} 42 \\ \times\ 30 \\ \hline \end{array}$

Step Up to Math · Intermediate · CD-104260 · © Carson-Dellosa

Multiplying by Two-Digit Numbers

To multiply by a two-digit number, follow these steps:

1. Multiply the top number by the ones digit in the second number. Regroup if necessary.

2. Write a zero in the ones column.

3. Multiply the top number by the tens digit in the second number. Regroup if necessary.

4. Add. Regroup if necessary.

```
  1 3
  229
x  34
  916
```

```
  1 3
  229
x  34
  916
    0
```

```
   2
  229
x  34
  916
+6,870
```

```
   2
  229
x  34
  916
+6,870
 7,786
```

Multiply.

1.   41
       x 32

2.   35
       x 24

3.   21
       x 34

4.   42
       x 16

5.   21
       x 52

6.   236
      x 31

7.   211
      x 25

8.   480
      x 12

9.   232
      x 44

10.   271
      x 18

11.   499
      x 35

12.   355
      x 29

13.   258
      x 72

14.   289
      x 13

15.   980
      x 20

Name: _____   Date: _____

Multiplying by Two-Digit Numbers

To multiply by a two-digit number, follow these steps:

1. Multiply the top number by the ones digit in the second number. Regroup if necessary.

$$\begin{array}{r} 1\ 3\ 3 \\ 1{,}378 \\ \times\quad 34 \\ \hline 5{,}512 \end{array}$$

2. Write a zero in the ones column.

$$\begin{array}{r} 1\ 3\ 3 \\ 1{,}378 \\ \times\quad 34 \\ \hline 5{,}512 \\ 0 \end{array}$$

3. Multiply the top number by the tens digit in the second number. Regroup if necessary.

$$\begin{array}{r} 1\ 2\ 2 \\ \cancel{1\ 3\ 3} \\ 1{,}378 \\ \times\quad 34 \\ \hline 5{,}512 \\ +\ 41{,}340 \end{array}$$

4. Add. Regroup if necessary.

$$\begin{array}{r} 1\ 2\ 2 \\ \cancel{1\ 3\ 3} \\ 1{,}378 \\ \times\quad 34 \\ \hline 5{,}512 \\ +\ 41{,}340 \\ \hline 46{,}852 \end{array}$$

Multiply.

1.   2,310
   x   24

2.   4,412
   x   35

3.   1,362
   x   28

4.   5,420
   x   41

5.   1,543
   x   23

6.   2,246
   x   51

7.   5,185
   x   43

8.   2,324
   x   81

9.   3,624
   x   27

10.   2,846
   x   34

11.   4,231
   x   55

12.   6,418
   x   23

Multiplying by Three-Digit Numbers

To multiply by a three-digit number, follow these steps:

1. Multiply the top number by the ones digit in the second number. Regroup if necessary. Write a zero in the ones column.

```
  318
x 200
-----
  000
    0
```

2. Multiply the top number by the tens digit in the second number. Regroup if necessary. Write a zero in the ones and tens columns.

```
  318
x 200
-----
  000
 0000
   00
```

3. Multiply the top number by the hundreds digit in the second number. Regroup if necessary. Add. Regroup if necessary.

```
     1
   318
 x 200
------
   000
  0000
+63,600
------
 63,600
```

Multiply.

1.   289
    x 300

2.   648
    x 200

3.   135
    x 200

4.   825
    x 400

5.   698
    x 400

6.   147
    x 300

7.   358
    x 500

8.   718
    x 300

Name: _____   Date: _____

Multiplying by Three-Digit Numbers

To multiply by a three-digit number, follow these steps:

1. Multiply the top number by the ones digit in the second number. Regroup if necessary. Write a zero in the ones column.

2. Multiply the top number by the tens digit in the second number. Regroup if necessary. Write zeros in the ones and tens columns.

3. Multiply the top number by the hundreds digit in the second number. Regroup if necessary. Add. Regroup if necessary.

```
      318
   x  230
   ------
      000
        0
```

```
       2
      318
   x  230
   ------
      000
    9,540
       00
```

```
      1
      318
   x  230
   ------
      000
    9,540
 + 63,600
 --------
   73,140
```

Multiply.

1.   364
     x 120

2.   378
     x 250

3.   354
     x 350

4.   671
     x 480

5.   500
     x 410

6.   534
     x 120

7.   439
     x 380

8.   266
     x 160

9.   180
     x 350

10.   911
      x 430

11.   236
      x 350

12.   741
      x 240

Step Up to Math · Intermediate · CD-104260 · © Carson-Dellosa

Name: _____   Date: _____

Multiplying by Three-Digit Numbers

To multiply by a three-digit number, follow these steps:

1. Multiply the top number by the ones digit in the second number. Regroup if necessary. Write a zero in the ones column.

2. Multiply the top number by the tens digit in the second number. Regroup if necessary. Write zeros in the ones and tens columns.

3. Multiply the top number by the hundreds digit in the second number. Regroup if necessary. Add. Regroup if necessary.

$$
\begin{array}{r}
\overset{3}{3}18 \\
\times\ 234 \\
\hline
1{,}272 \\
0
\end{array}
$$

$$
\begin{array}{r}
\overset{2}{\cancel{8}}18 \\
\times\ 234 \\
\hline
1{,}272 \\
9{,}540 \\
00
\end{array}
$$

$$
\begin{array}{r}
\overset{1}{\cancel{\cancel{8}}}18 \\
\times\ 234 \\
\hline
1{,}272 \\
9{,}540 \\
+\ 63{,}600 \\
\hline
74{,}412
\end{array}
$$

Multiply.

1. 123
    x 315

2. 209
    x 354

3. 352
    x 418

4. 295
    x 342

5. 302
    x 418

6. 204
    x 389

7. 285
    x 725

8. 246
    x 319

9. 843
    x 310

10. 749
    x 123

11. 603
    x 123

12. 549
    x 256

13. 816
    x 249

14. 304
    x 203

15. 220
    x 649

Basic Division Facts

Dividing separates numbers into groups. A **quotient** is the answer to a division problem. Division looks like this:

Total Number   Number of groups   Number in each group

$$12 \div 3 = 4$$

Divided by   Equals

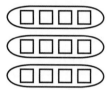

Divide. Draw pictures to help find each quotient.

1. $10 \div 5 = \boxed{}$

2. $15 \div 3 = \boxed{}$

3. $6 \div 3 = \boxed{}$

4. $8 \div 2 = \boxed{}$

5. $9 \div 3 = \boxed{}$

6. $20 \div 4 = \boxed{}$

7. $12 \div 6 = \boxed{}$

8. $18 \div 3 = \boxed{}$

9. $14 \div 7 = \boxed{}$

10. $25 \div 5 = \boxed{}$

11. $16 \div 8 = \boxed{}$

12. $10 \div 2 = \boxed{}$

Basic Division Facts

A **dividend** is the number being divided. A **divisor** is the number by which the dividend is divided. A **quotient** is the answer to a division problem.

dividend   divisor   quotient

$$12 \div 3 = 4$$

divisor $\quad$ 4 ← quotient

$$3\overline{)12}$$ ← dividend

Knowing how to multiply can help you divide. Ask yourself: What number multiplied by the divisor equals the dividend? 3 x ____ = 12   3 x 4 = 12

Divide. Use multiplication to help find each quotient.

1. $12 \div 6 =$ ☐

2. $24 \div 4 =$ ☐

3. $40 \div 5 =$ ☐

4. $16 \div 4 =$ ☐

5. $21 \div 7 =$ ☐

6. $9 \div 3 =$ ☐

7. $36 \div 6 =$ ☐

8. $24 \div 8 =$ ☐

9. $20 \div 4 =$ ☐

10. $15 \div 5 =$ ☐

11. $12 \div 4 =$ ☐

12. $25 \div 5 =$ ☐

13. $9\overline{)27}$

14. $9\overline{)36}$

15. $9\overline{)81}$

16. $6\overline{)54}$

17. $9\overline{)63}$

18. $5\overline{)45}$

19. $7\overline{)56}$

20. $7\overline{)49}$

Basic Division Facts

A **dividend** is the number being divided. A **divisor** is the number by which the dividend is divided. A **quotient** is the answer to a division problem.

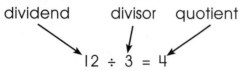

dividend   divisor   quotient

$12 \div 3 = 4$

divisor $\overset{4}{)\overline{12}}$ ← quotient
3$)\overline{12}$ ← dividend

Knowing how to multiply can help you divide. Ask yourself: What number multiplied by the divisor equals the dividend? 3 x ____ = 12   3 x 4 = 12

Divide. Then, match the quotients to the numbers below and fill in the correct letters.

W	T	I	F
1. $7)\overline{42}$	2. $9)\overline{9}$	3. $6)\overline{30}$	4. $5)\overline{40}$
A	**S**	**L**	**R**
5. $8)\overline{56}$	6. $3)\overline{27}$	7. $8)\overline{80}$	8. $8)\overline{16}$
K	**E**		
9. $9)\overline{36}$	10. $7)\overline{21}$		

The first bicycles had no pedals. People walked them along until they came to a hill. Then, they rode down the hill.

What was the first bicycle called?

___ ___ ___ ___ ___ ___ ___ ___ ___ ___ ___ ___
7   9   6   5   8   1   6   7   10   4   3   2

Dividing without Remainders

Sometimes, the number being divided is larger than the basic facts you have learned. To divide large numbers, follow these steps:

1. Try to divide the tens digit of the dividend by the divisor.

2. Write this quotient above the tens digit. Multiply the divisor by this quotient. Write the product under the tens digit.

3. Subtract to find the remainder.

4. Bring down the ones place of the dividend. Divide the divisor into this number. Subtract.

$$
4\overline{)56}
\qquad
\begin{array}{r} 1 \\ 4\overline{)56} \\ -4 \end{array}
\qquad
\begin{array}{r} 1 \\ 4\overline{)56} \\ -4 \\ \hline 1 \end{array}
\qquad
\begin{array}{r} 14 \\ 4\overline{)56} \\ -4 \\ \hline 16 \\ -16 \\ \hline 0 \end{array}
$$

Divide.

1. $3\overline{)66}$

2. $2\overline{)98}$

3. $5\overline{)90}$

4. $7\overline{)84}$

5. $5\overline{)75}$

6. $3\overline{)87}$

7. $8\overline{)96}$

8. $2\overline{)76}$

9. $6\overline{)84}$

10. $3\overline{)54}$

11. $4\overline{)96}$

12. $5\overline{)85}$

Dividing without Remainders

When dividing into two-digit dividends, follow these steps:

1. Try to divide the tens digit of the dividend by the divisor.

2. Write this quotient above the tens digit. Multiply the divisor by this quotient. Write the product under the tens digit.

3. Subtract to find the remainder.

4. Bring down the ones place of the dividend. Divide the divisor into this number. Subtract.

$3\overline{)42}$

$\begin{array}{r} 1 \\ 3\overline{)42} \\ -3 \end{array}$

$\begin{array}{r} 1 \\ 3\overline{)42} \\ -3 \\ \hline 1 \end{array}$

$\begin{array}{r} 14 \\ 3\overline{)42} \\ -3 \\ \hline 12 \\ -12 \\ \hline 0 \end{array}$

Divide.

1. $4\overline{)84}$ 2. $3\overline{)96}$ 3. $3\overline{)63}$ 4. $2\overline{)68}$

5. $6\overline{)78}$ 6. $5\overline{)90}$ 7. $3\overline{)75}$ 8. $5\overline{)65}$

9. $3\overline{)51}$ 10. $7\overline{)84}$ 11. $4\overline{)64}$ 12. $2\overline{)56}$

13. $4\overline{)76}$ 14. $6\overline{)72}$ 15. $8\overline{)96}$ 16. $2\overline{)76}$

Name: _____   Date: _____

Dividing without Remainders

When dividing into three-digit dividends, follow these steps:

1. Try to divide the hundreds digit of the dividend by the divisor. You cannot.

$$6\overline{)534}$$

2. Divide into the hundreds and tens places of the dividend. Multiply the divisor by the quotient.

$$\begin{array}{r} 8 \\ 6\overline{)534} \\ -48 \end{array}$$

3. Subtract to find the remainder.

$$\begin{array}{r} 8 \\ 6\overline{)534} \\ -48 \\ \hline 5 \end{array}$$

4. Bring down the ones place of the dividend. Divide the divisor into this number. Subtract.

$$\begin{array}{r} 89 \\ 6\overline{)534} \\ -48 \\ \hline 54 \\ -54 \\ \hline 0 \end{array}$$

Divide.

1. $2\overline{)196}$ 2. $5\overline{)335}$ 3. $7\overline{)476}$ 4. $3\overline{)273}$

5. $6\overline{)204}$ 6. $8\overline{)624}$ 7. $7\overline{)182}$ 8. $4\overline{)292}$

9. $8\overline{)464}$ 10. $4\overline{)324}$ 11. $6\overline{)576}$ 12. $3\overline{)141}$

13. $6\overline{)174}$ 14. $5\overline{)240}$ 15. $9\overline{)243}$ 16. $8\overline{)232}$

Name: _____   Date: _____

Dividing with Remainders

Sometimes when dividing, there is a number left over. This number is called a **remainder**. To find a remainder, follow these steps:

1. Try to divide the tens digit of the dividend by the divisor. You cannot.

2. Divide into the ones and tens places. Multiply the divisor by the quotient. Write the product under the ones and tens digits.

3. Subtract to find the remainder. Check if the divisor can be divided into this number.

4. It cannot, so that number is written as a remainder.

$$4\overline{)18}$$

$$\begin{array}{r} 4 \\ 4\overline{)18} \\ -16 \end{array}$$

$$\begin{array}{r} 4 \\ 4\overline{)18} \\ -16 \\ \hline 2 \end{array}$$

$$\begin{array}{r} 4\ R2 \\ 4\overline{)18} \\ -16 \\ \hline 2 \end{array}$$

Divide.

1. $8\overline{)34}$ 2. $4\overline{)26}$ 3. $7\overline{)67}$ 4. $3\overline{)17}$

5. $9\overline{)29}$ 6. $5\overline{)42}$ 7. $6\overline{)47}$ 8. $9\overline{)83}$

9. $6\overline{)39}$ 10. $4\overline{)19}$ 11. $5\overline{)24}$ 12. $8\overline{)79}$

13. $7\overline{)41}$ 14. $6\overline{)23}$ 15. $9\overline{)60}$ 16. $4\overline{)15}$

Name: _____   Date: _____

Dividing with Remainders

Sometimes when dividing, there is a number left over. This number is called a **remainder**. To find a remainder, follow these steps:

1. Try to divide the tens digit of the dividend by the divisor. You cannot.

2. Divide into the ones and tens places. Multiply the divisor by the quotient. Write the product under the ones and tens digits.

3. Subtract to find the remainder. Check if the divisor can be divided into this number.

4. It cannot, so that number is written as a remainder.

$$7 \overline{)51}$$

$$\begin{array}{r} 7 \\ 7 \overline{)51} \\ -49 \end{array}$$

$$\begin{array}{r} 7 \\ 7 \overline{)51} \\ -49 \\ \hline 2 \end{array}$$

$$\begin{array}{r} 7 \text{ R2} \\ 7 \overline{)51} \\ -49 \\ \hline 2 \end{array}$$

Divide.

1. $5 \overline{)27}$ 2. $2 \overline{)17}$ 3. $6 \overline{)25}$ 4. $7 \overline{)23}$

5. $4 \overline{)19}$ 6. $9 \overline{)84}$ 7. $6 \overline{)39}$ 8. $8 \overline{)20}$

9. $5 \overline{)48}$ 10. $9 \overline{)30}$ 11. $6 \overline{)35}$ 12. $4 \overline{)35}$

13. $5 \overline{)19}$ 14. $9 \overline{)50}$ 15. $7 \overline{)44}$ 16. $3 \overline{)17}$

Name: _____ Date: _____

Dividing with Remainders

Sometimes when dividing, there is a number left over. This number is called a **remainder**. To find a remainder, follow these steps:

1. Try to divide the hundreds digit of the dividend by the divisor. You cannot.

2. Divide into the hundreds and tens places of the dividend. Multiply the divisor by the quotient. Subtract.

3. Bring down the ones place of the dividend. Divide the divisor into this number. Subtract.

4. Check if the divisor can be divided into the remaining number. It cannot, so that number is written as a remainder.

$6\overline{)253}$

$\begin{array}{r} 4 \\ 6\overline{)253} \\ -24 \\ \hline 1 \end{array}$

$\begin{array}{r} 4 \\ 6\overline{)253} \\ -24 \\ \hline 13 \\ -12 \\ \hline 1 \end{array}$

$\begin{array}{r} 42\,R1 \\ 6\overline{)253} \\ -24 \\ \hline 13 \\ -12 \\ \hline 1 \end{array}$

Divide.

1. $2\overline{)119}$ 2. $4\overline{)227}$ 3. $5\overline{)444}$ 4. $3\overline{)337}$

5. $6\overline{)445}$ 6. $7\overline{)660}$ 7. $8\overline{)775}$ 8. $6\overline{)251}$

9. $7\overline{)169}$ 10. $4\overline{)335}$ 11. $3\overline{)520}$ 12. $9\overline{)680}$

Name: _____   Date: _____

More Division with Remainders

Example:

1. Can 6 be divided into 8? Yes.

$$6\overline{)89}$$

2. Divide and subtract. Bring down the 9.

$$\begin{array}{r} 1 \\ 6\overline{)89} \\ -6 \\ \hline 29 \end{array}$$

3. Can 6 be divided into 29? Yes.

$$\begin{array}{r} 1 \\ 6\overline{)89} \\ -6 \\ \hline 29 \end{array}$$

4. Divide and subtract. Five is the remainder.

$$\begin{array}{r} 14\ R5 \\ 6\overline{)89} \\ -6 \\ \hline 29 \\ -24 \\ \hline 5 \end{array}$$

Divide.

1. $3\overline{)89}$ 2. $4\overline{)78}$ 3. $2\overline{)97}$ 4. $8\overline{)93}$

5. $7\overline{)94}$ 6. $3\overline{)77}$ 7. $2\overline{)71}$ 8. $5\overline{)76}$

9. $6\overline{)85}$ 10. $5\overline{)98}$ 11. $4\overline{)90}$ 12. $3\overline{)73}$

More Division with Remainders

Example:

1. Can 6 be divided into 2?
No.

$$6\overline{)253}$$

2. Divide 6 into 25. Subtract. Bring down the 3.

$$\begin{array}{r} 4 \\ 6\overline{)253} \\ -24 \\ \hline 13 \end{array}$$

3. Can 6 be divided into 13?
Yes.

$$\begin{array}{r} 4 \\ 6\overline{)253} \\ -24 \\ \hline 13 \end{array}$$

4. Divide and subtract. One is the remainder.

$$\begin{array}{r} 42\,R1 \\ 6\overline{)253} \\ -24 \\ \hline 13 \\ -12 \\ \hline 1 \end{array}$$

Divide.

1. $3\overline{)41}$

2. $5\overline{)59}$

3. $2\overline{)71}$

4. $7\overline{)80}$

5. $4\overline{)91}$

6. $4\overline{)89}$

7. $2\overline{)93}$

8. $3\overline{)47}$

9. $8\overline{)982}$

10. $6\overline{)794}$

11. $5\overline{)792}$

12. $7\overline{)951}$

Step Up to Math · Intermediate · CD-104260 · © Carson-Dellosa

More Division with Remainders

Example:

1. Can 7 be divided into 5? No.

$$7\overline{)586}$$

2. Divide 7 into 58. Subtract. Bring down the 6.

$$\begin{array}{r} 8 \\ 7\overline{)586} \\ -56 \\ \hline 26 \end{array}$$

3. Can 7 be divided into 26? Yes.

$$\begin{array}{r} 8 \\ 7\overline{)586} \\ -56 \\ \hline 26 \end{array}$$

4. Divide and subtract. Five is the remainder.

$$\begin{array}{r} 83\ R5 \\ 7\overline{)586} \\ -56 \\ \hline 26 \\ -21 \\ \hline 5 \end{array}$$

Divide.

1. $4\overline{)317}$

2. $6\overline{)351}$

3. $5\overline{)214}$

4. $8\overline{)511}$

5. $7\overline{)200}$

6. $4\overline{)159}$

7. $6\overline{)166}$

8. $3\overline{)290}$

9. $4\overline{)291}$

10. $6\overline{)173}$

11. $7\overline{)552}$

12. $3\overline{)292}$

Zeros in the Quotient

Example:

1. Can 3 be divided into 2? No.

$$3\overline{)270}$$

2. Divide 3 into 27. Subtract. Bring down the 0.

$$\begin{array}{r} 9 \\ 3\overline{)270} \\ -27 \\ \hline 00 \end{array}$$

3. Can 3 be divided into 0? No.

$$\begin{array}{r} 9 \\ 3\overline{)270} \\ -27 \\ \hline 00 \end{array}$$

4. Write a 0 in the ones place.

$$\begin{array}{r} 90 \\ 3\overline{)270} \\ -27 \\ \hline 00 \\ -0 \\ \hline 0 \end{array}$$

Divide.

1. $2\overline{)200}$

2. $7\overline{)350}$

3. $8\overline{)720}$

4. $8\overline{)400}$

5. $9\overline{)810}$

6. $7\overline{)630}$

7. $7\overline{)210}$

8. $7\overline{)420}$

9. $9\overline{)540}$

10. $6\overline{)300}$

11. $3\overline{)240}$

12. $4\overline{)160}$

Zeros in the Quotient

Example:

1. Can 7 be divided into 7? Yes. Divide and subtract. Bring down the 4.

$$\begin{array}{r} 1 \\ 7\overline{)748} \\ -7 \\ \hline 04 \end{array}$$

2. Can 7 be divided into 4? No. Write a 0 in the tens place. Bring down the 8.

$$\begin{array}{r} 10 \\ 7\overline{)748} \\ -7 \\ \hline 048 \end{array}$$

3. Can 7 be divided into 48? Yes. Divide and subtract.

$$\begin{array}{r} 106 \\ 7\overline{)748} \\ -7 \\ \hline 048 \\ -42 \\ \hline 6 \end{array}$$

4. Can 7 be divided into 6? No. Six is the remainder.

$$\begin{array}{r} 106 \text{ R6} \\ 7\overline{)748} \\ -7 \\ \hline 048 \\ -42 \\ \hline 6 \end{array}$$

Divide.

1. $3\overline{)925}$

2. $5\overline{)904}$

3. $2\overline{)813}$

4. $4\overline{)839}$

5. $7\overline{)985}$

6. $6\overline{)656}$

7. $8\overline{)966}$

8. $4\overline{)434}$

9. $2\overline{)681}$

10. $4\overline{)762}$

11. $2\overline{)811}$

12. $5\overline{)519}$

Zeros in the Quotient

Example:

1. Can 4 be divided into 1? No.

$$4\overline{)1{,}227}$$

2. Divide 4 into 12. Subtract. Bring down the 2.

$$\begin{array}{r} 3 \\ 4\overline{)1{,}227} \\ -12 \\ \hline 02 \end{array}$$

3. Can 4 be divided into 2? No. Write a 0 in the tens place. Bring down the 7. Divide and subtract.

$$\begin{array}{r} 306 \\ 4\overline{)1{,}227} \\ -12 \\ \hline 027 \\ -24 \\ \hline 3 \end{array}$$

4. Can 4 be divided into 3? No. Three is the remainder.

$$\begin{array}{r} 306\ R3 \\ 4\overline{)1{,}227} \\ -12 \\ \hline 027 \\ -24 \\ \hline 3 \end{array}$$

Divide.

1. $4\overline{)203}$

2. $3\overline{)1{,}208}$

3. $2\overline{)1{,}601}$

4. $5\overline{)546}$

5. $2\overline{)811}$

6. $7\overline{)725}$

7. $9\overline{)278}$

8. $5\overline{)1{,}549}$

9. $3\overline{)2{,}120}$

10. $6\overline{)1{,}235}$

11. $4\overline{)3{,}631}$

12. $6\overline{)650}$

Dividing by Two-Digit Numbers

To divide by two-digit numbers, follow these steps:

1. Can 20 be divided into 12? No.

$$20\overline{)120}$$

2. Divide 20 into 120. Find a number that, when multiplied by 20, equals 120.

$$20\overline{)120}$$

3. Place a 6 in the quotient. Multiply 6 x 20. Subtract.

$$\begin{array}{r} 6 \\ 20\overline{)120} \\ -\ 120 \\ \hline 0 \end{array}$$

Divide.

1. $10\overline{)50}$
2. $30\overline{)120}$
3. $40\overline{)200}$
4. $10\overline{)100}$
5. $20\overline{)180}$

6. $40\overline{)160}$
7. $30\overline{)240}$
8. $50\overline{)400}$
9. $20\overline{)80}$
10. $60\overline{)600}$

11. $30\overline{)150}$
12. $70\overline{)350}$
13. $80\overline{)160}$
14. $30\overline{)210}$
15. $10\overline{)70}$

Name: _____ Date: _____

Dividing by Two-Digit Numbers

To divide by two-digit numbers, follow these steps:

1. Can 30 be divided into 25? No. Can 30 be divided into 256. Yes. Round 256 to a number divisible by 30.

2. $270 \div 30 = 9$. Since $270 > 256$, round down. $240 \div 30 = 8$. Eight is the partial quotient.

3. Multiply 8 x 30. Subtract. Bring down the 7. Divide 30 into 167.

4. Multiply 5 x 30. Subtract. Can 30 be divided into 17? No. Seventeen is the remainder.

$$30\overline{)2{,}567}$$

$$\begin{array}{r} 8 \\ 30\overline{)2{,}567} \end{array}$$

$$\begin{array}{r} 8 \\ 30\overline{)2{,}567} \\ -240 \\ \hline 167 \end{array}$$

$$\begin{array}{r} 85\ R17 \\ 30\overline{)2{,}567} \\ -2\,40 \\ \hline 167 \\ -150 \\ \hline 17 \end{array}$$

Divide.

1. $30\overline{)438}$

2. $20\overline{)696}$

3. $40\overline{)925}$

4. $30\overline{)518}$

5. $20\overline{)756}$

6. $40\overline{)1{,}308}$

7. $80\overline{)1{,}712}$

8. $60\overline{)856}$

9. $50\overline{)1{,}585}$

10. $70\overline{)952}$

11. $20\overline{)827}$

12. $40\overline{)874}$

Step Up to Math · Intermediate · CD-104260 · © Carson-Dellosa

Dividing by Two-Digit Numbers

To divide by two-digit numbers, follow these steps:

1. Can 24 be divided into 13? No. Can 24 be divided into 136? Yes. Round 136 to a number divisible by 24.

$$24\overline{)1{,}367}$$

2. $120 \div 24 = 5$. Since $120 < 136$, 5 is the partial quotient. Multiply 5×24. Subtract.

$$\begin{array}{r} 5 \\ 24\overline{)1{,}367} \\ -120 \\ \hline 16 \end{array}$$

3. Bring down the 7. Divide 24 into 167.

$$\begin{array}{r} 5 \\ 24\overline{)1{,}367} \\ -120 \\ \hline 167 \end{array}$$

4. Multiply 6×24. Subtract. Can 24 be divided into 23? No. Twenty-three is the remainder.

$$\begin{array}{r} 56\,R23 \\ 24\overline{)1{,}367} \\ -120 \\ \hline 167 \\ -144 \\ \hline 23 \end{array}$$

Divide.

1. $16\overline{)6{,}889}$

2. $32\overline{)1{,}798}$

3. $21\overline{)6{,}292}$

4. $41\overline{)1{,}596}$

5. $81\overline{)1{,}155}$

6. $42\overline{)1{,}532}$

7. $51\overline{)1{,}468}$

8. $72\overline{)1{,}562}$

9. $14\overline{)5{,}184}$

Name: _____   Date: _____

Finding Fractions

To find fractions of a whole and a set, ask yourself these questions:

Fractions of a whole

 $\dfrac{4}{8}$ numerator
denominator

How many parts are shaded?
4 (numerator)

How many parts is this whole figure divided into? 8 (denominator)

Fractions of a set

△■●△■● $\dfrac{6}{12}$ numerator
△□○△□○ denominator

How many figures are shaded?
6 (numerator)

How many figures are there in the set in all? 12 (denominator)

What fraction of each whole figure is shaded?

1.

2.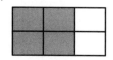

3.

4.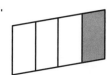

5.

_____   _____   _____   _____   _____

6.

7.

8.

9.

10.

_____   _____   _____   _____   _____

What fraction of each set is shaded?

11.

12.

13.

14.

15.

_____   _____   _____   _____   _____

    Step Up to Math · **Intermediate** · **CD-104260** · © **Carson-Dellosa**

Finding Fractions

Fractions can be used to describe the parts of a matching set. If the sets are too large to draw pictures, division can be used to find the part of a set described by the fraction.

Example: Find $\frac{1}{3}$ of 12.

This means divide 12 into 3 equal parts.

$12 \div 3 = 4$ $\frac{1}{3}$ of 12 = 4

Divide to find each answer.

1. $\frac{1}{3}$ of 21 =

2. $\frac{1}{8}$ of 24 =

3. $\frac{1}{6}$ of 36 =

4. $\frac{1}{2}$ of 18 =

5. $\frac{1}{3}$ of 15 =

6. $\frac{1}{5}$ of 25 =

7. $\frac{1}{4}$ of 16 =

8. $\frac{1}{3}$ of 9 =

9. $\frac{1}{7}$ of 49 =

10. $\frac{1}{9}$ of 27 =

11. $\frac{1}{6}$ of 42 =

12. $\frac{1}{5}$ of 45 =

Name: _____ Date: _____

Finding Fractions

Fractions can be used to describe the parts of a matching set. If the sets are too large to draw pictures, division can be used to find the part of a set described by the fraction.

Example: Find $\frac{1}{4}$ of 28.

This means to divide 28 into 4 equal parts.

$28 \div 4 = 7$ $\frac{1}{4}$ of 28 = 7

Divide to find each answer.

1. $\frac{1}{3}$ of 15 =   2. $\frac{1}{6}$ of 12 =   3. $\frac{1}{2}$ of 10 =   4. $\frac{1}{4}$ of 20 =

5. $\frac{1}{7}$ of 14 =   6. $\frac{1}{8}$ of 24 =   7. $\frac{1}{7}$ of 28 =   8. $\frac{1}{3}$ of 27 =

9. $\frac{1}{5}$ of 30 =   10. $\frac{1}{8}$ of 40 =   11. $\frac{1}{4}$ of 36 =   12. $\frac{1}{5}$ of 10 =

13. $\frac{1}{5}$ of 45 =   14. $\frac{1}{3}$ of 21 =   15. $\frac{1}{6}$ of 12 =   16. $\frac{1}{10}$ of 20 =

Finding Equivalent Fractions

Fractions that equal the same amount are called **equivalent fractions**.

Example:

$$\frac{1}{2} = \frac{2}{4}$$

Write the equivalent fractions.

    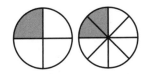

1. ____ = ____   2. ____ = ____   3. ____ = ____

    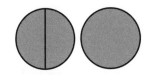

4. ____ = ____   5. ____ = ____   6. ____ = ____

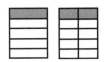   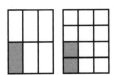   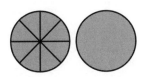

7. ____ = ____   8. ____ = ____   9. ____ = ____

   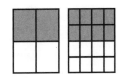   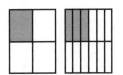

10. ____ = ____   11. ____ = ____   12. ____ = ____

Name: _____ Date: _____

Finding Equivalent Fractions

When adding or subtracting fractions with different denominators, you will need to use the **least common denominator** to find an equivalent fraction. The least common denominator (**LCD**) is the smallest number divisible by each denominator. To find equivalent fractions using the LCD, follow these steps:

1. List the multiples of each denominator.

$\frac{1}{3}$

3 x 0 = 0
3 x 1 = 3
3 x 2 = 6
3 x 3 = 9
3 x 4 = 12
3 x 5 = 15
3 x 6 = 18

$\frac{1}{5}$

5 x 0 = 0
5 x 1 = 5
5 x 2 = 10
5 x 3 = 15
5 x 4 = 20
5 x 5 = 25
5 x 6 = 30

2. Find the smallest number, other than 0, that appears in each list. In this example, it is 15. This is the LCD.

3. Find the number you must multiply the denominator by to make it equal to the LCD, and multiply the numerator by that same number. In this example, $\frac{1}{3}$ is multiplied by $\frac{5}{5}$ and $\frac{1}{5}$ is multiplied by $\frac{3}{3}$. (Note that $\frac{5}{5}$ and $\frac{3}{3}$ equal 1, so the fractions are still equal, but they are written a different way.)

$$\frac{1 \times 5}{3 \times 5} = \frac{5}{15}$$

$$\frac{1 \times 3}{5 \times 3} = \frac{3}{15}$$

Find the least common denominator and equivalent fractions for each pair of fractions. List the multiples of each denominator on another sheet of paper to help find the LCD.

1. $\frac{1}{2} =$ $\frac{1}{5} =$

   LCD = _____

2. $\frac{1}{2} =$ $\frac{1}{3} =$

   LCD = _____

3. $\frac{1}{3} =$ $\frac{1}{8} =$

   LCD = _____

4. $\frac{1}{2} =$ $\frac{1}{7} =$

   LCD = _____

5. $\frac{1}{3} =$ $\frac{1}{4} =$

   LCD = _____

6. $\frac{1}{2} =$ $\frac{1}{9} =$

   LCD = _____

Finding Equivalent Fractions

When adding or subtracting fractions with different denominators, you will need to use the **least common denominator** to find an equivalent fraction. The least common denominator (**LCD**) is the smallest number divisible by each denominator. To find equivalent fractions using the LCD, follow these steps:

1. List the multiples of each denominator.

$$\frac{1}{4}$$

$4 \times 0 = \boxed{0}$
$4 \times 1 = 4$
$4 \times 2 = 8$
$4 \times 3 = 12$
$4 \times 4 = 16$
$4 \times 5 = 20$
$4 \times 6 = 24$

$$\frac{1}{5}$$

$5 \times 0 = \boxed{0}$
$5 \times 1 = 5$
$5 \times 2 = 10$
$5 \times 3 = 15$
$5 \times 4 = 20$
$5 \times 5 = 25$
$5 \times 6 = 30$

2. Find the smallest number, other than 0, that appears in each list. In this example, it is 20. This is the LCD.

3. Find the number you must multiply the denominator by to make it equal to the LCD, and multiply the numerator by that same number. In this example, $\frac{1}{4}$ is multiplied by $\frac{5}{5}$ and $\frac{1}{5}$ is multiplied by $\frac{4}{4}$. (Note that $\frac{5}{5}$ and $\frac{4}{4}$ equal 1, so the fractions are still equal, but they are written a different way.)

$$\frac{1 \times 5}{4 \times 5} = \frac{5}{20}$$

$$\frac{1 \times 4}{5 \times 4} = \frac{4}{20}$$

Find the least common denominator and equivalent fractions for each pair of fractions. List the multiples of each denominator on another sheet of paper to help find the LCD.

1. $\frac{1}{4} =$ $\frac{1}{6} =$

   LCD = _____

2. $\frac{1}{3} =$ $\frac{1}{7} =$

   LCD = _____

3. $\frac{1}{5} =$ $\frac{1}{6} =$

   LCD = _____

4. $\frac{1}{6} =$ $\frac{1}{7} =$

   LCD = _____

5. $\frac{1}{4} =$ $\frac{1}{7} =$

   LCD = _____

6. $\frac{1}{3} =$ $\frac{1}{5} =$

   LCD = _____

Reducing Fractions

Some fractions can be **reduced**. A reduced fraction is an equivalent fraction that uses the smallest numbers possible. Follow these steps to reduce a fraction:

1. Find the largest number that can be divided into both the numerator and the denominator. In this example, it is 3.

$$\frac{9}{12}$$

$9 \div 1 = \boxed{9}$ $12 \div 1 = \boxed{12}$
$9 \div 3 = \boxed{3}$ $12 \div 2 = 6$
$9 \div 9 = \boxed{1}$ $12 \div 3 = 4$
                         $12 \div 4 = 3$
                         $12 \div 6 = 2$
                         $12 \div 12 = 1$

2. Divide both the numerator and denominator by this number.

$$\frac{9}{12} \div \frac{3}{3} = \frac{3}{4}$$

$$\frac{9}{12} = \frac{3}{4}$$

Divide to reduce each fraction.

1. $\dfrac{6}{12} \div {} =$

2. $\dfrac{4}{10} \div {} =$

3. $\dfrac{10}{15} \div {} =$

4. $\dfrac{3}{9} \div {} =$

5. $\dfrac{8}{12} \div {} =$

6. $\dfrac{14}{18} \div {} =$

   Step Up to Math   ·   Intermediate   ·   CD-104260   ·   © Carson-Dellosa

Reducing Fractions

Some fractions can be **reduced**. A reduced fraction is an equivalent fraction that is written in lowest terms. To reduce a fraction, find the **greatest common factor**. The greatest common factor is the largest number that divides evenly into the numerator and denominator. Follow these steps to reduce a fraction:

1. Find the greatest common factor. In this example, it is 6.

$$\frac{6}{12}$$

$6 \div 1 = \boxed{6}$
$6 \div 2 = \boxed{3}$
$6 \div 3 = \boxed{2}$
$6 \div 6 = \boxed{1}$

$12 \div 1 = \boxed{12}$
$12 \div 2 = \boxed{6}$
$12 \div 3 = \boxed{4}$
$12 \div 4 = \boxed{3}$
$12 \div 6 = \boxed{2}$
$12 \div 12 = \boxed{1}$

2. Divide both the numerator and denominator by this number.

$$\frac{6}{12} \div \frac{6}{6} = \frac{1}{2}$$

$$\frac{6}{12} = \frac{1}{2}$$

Reduce each fraction to lowest terms.

1. $\frac{10}{12}$ =

2. $\frac{4}{16}$ =

3. $\frac{6}{18}$ =

4. $\frac{10}{30}$ =

5. $\frac{14}{16}$ =

6. $\frac{7}{35}$ =

7. $\frac{5}{15}$ =

8. $\frac{4}{20}$ =

9. $\frac{9}{18}$ =

Name: _____   Date: _____

Reducing Fractions

Some fractions can be **reduced**. A reduced fraction is an equivalent fraction that is written in lowest terms. To reduce a fraction, find the **greatest common factor**. The greatest common factor is the largest number that divides evenly into the numerator and denominator. Follow these steps to reduce a fraction:

1. Find the greatest common factor. In this example, it is 6.

$$\frac{6}{12}$$

$6 \div 1 = \boxed{6}$
$6 \div 2 = \boxed{3}$
$6 \div 3 = \boxed{2}$
$6 \div 6 = \boxed{1}$

$12 \div 1 = \boxed{12}$
$12 \div 2 = \boxed{6}$
$12 \div 3 = \boxed{4}$
$12 \div 4 = \boxed{3}$
$12 \div 6 = \boxed{2}$
$12 \div 12 = \boxed{1}$

2. Divide the numerator and denominator by this number.

$$\frac{6}{12} \div \frac{6}{6} = \frac{1}{2}$$

$$\frac{6}{12} = \frac{1}{2}$$

Reduce each fraction to lowest terms.

1. $\dfrac{8}{24} =$

2. $\dfrac{8}{26} =$

3. $\dfrac{10}{16} =$

4. $\dfrac{12}{14} =$

5. $\dfrac{5}{25} =$

6. $\dfrac{10}{36} =$

7. $\dfrac{9}{24} =$

8. $\dfrac{6}{36} =$

9. $\dfrac{12}{30} =$

10. $\dfrac{8}{40} =$

11. $\dfrac{6}{27} =$

12. $\dfrac{2}{22} =$

Adding and Subtracting Fractions

To add or subtract fractions, the denominators must be the same. To add or subtract a fraction, follow these steps:

1. Are the denominators the same? Yes.

$$\frac{3}{8} + \frac{1}{8} =$$

$$\frac{3}{8} - \frac{1}{8} =$$

2. Add or subtract the numerators. Keep the same denominator.

$$\frac{3}{8} + \frac{1}{8} = \frac{4}{8}$$

$$\frac{3}{8} - \frac{1}{8} = \frac{2}{8}$$

3. Reduce to lowest terms.

$$\frac{4 \div 4}{8 \div 4} = \frac{1}{2}$$

$$\frac{2 \div 2}{8 \div 2} = \frac{1}{4}$$

Add or subtract. Reduce each answer to lowest terms.

1. $\frac{2}{4} + \frac{1}{4} =$

2. $\frac{6}{8} - \frac{4}{8} =$

3. $\frac{1}{5} + \frac{3}{5} =$

4. $\frac{4}{10} + \frac{5}{10} =$

5. $\frac{7}{8} - \frac{5}{8} =$

6. $\frac{9}{10} - \frac{3}{10} =$

7. $\frac{6}{9} + \frac{2}{9} =$

8. $\frac{10}{12} - \frac{6}{12} =$

9. $\frac{15}{20} - \frac{7}{20} =$

10. $\frac{68}{100} + \frac{12}{100} =$

11. $\frac{5}{50} + \frac{15}{50} =$

12. $\frac{12}{15} - \frac{9}{15} =$

Name: _____   Date: _____

Adding and Subtracting Fractions

To add or subtract fractions, the denominators must be the same. To add or subtract a fraction, follow these steps:

1. Are the denominators the same? Yes.

$$\frac{4}{9}$$
$$+\frac{2}{9}$$

2. Add or subtract the numerators. Keep the same denominator.

$$\frac{4}{9}$$
$$+\frac{2}{9}$$
$$\frac{6}{9}$$

3. Reduce to lowest terms.

$$\frac{6 \div 3}{9 \div 3} = \frac{2}{3}$$

Add or subtract. Reduce each answer to lowest terms.

1. $\frac{3}{7} - \frac{2}{7}$

2. $\frac{3}{9} + \frac{4}{9}$

3. $\frac{2}{14} + \frac{7}{14}$

4. $\frac{5}{10} - \frac{3}{10}$

5. $\frac{4}{11} + \frac{5}{11}$

6. $\frac{2}{8} + \frac{4}{8}$

7. $\frac{4}{5} - \frac{3}{5}$

8. $\frac{5}{9} - \frac{2}{9}$

9. $\frac{4}{15} + \frac{2}{15}$

10. $\frac{5}{13} - \frac{2}{13}$

11. $\frac{5}{8} - \frac{3}{8}$

12. $\frac{3}{10} + \frac{1}{10}$

Step Up to Math · Intermediate · CD-104260 · © Carson-Dellosa

Name: _____ Date: _____

Adding and Subtracting Fractions

To add or subtract fractions, the denominators must be the same. If the denominators are different, find the equivalent fractions with the least common denominator and then add or subtract. To add or subtract with different denominators, follow these steps:

1. Find the least common denominator and equivalent fractions if necessary.

$$\frac{2}{3} = \frac{4}{6}$$
$$-\frac{2}{6} = -\frac{2}{6}$$

2. Add or subtract the numerators. Keep the same denominator.

$$\frac{4}{6}$$
$$-\frac{2}{6}$$
$$\frac{2}{6}$$

3. Reduce to lowest terms.

$$\frac{2 \div 2}{6 \div 2} = \frac{1}{3}$$

Add or subtract. Reduce each answer to lowest terms.

1. $\frac{3}{4} + \frac{1}{8}$

2. $\frac{5}{7} - \frac{3}{14}$

3. $\frac{4}{4} - \frac{3}{6}$

4. $\frac{7}{11} + \frac{3}{11}$

5. $\frac{3}{4} - \frac{2}{3}$

6. $\frac{6}{12} + \frac{3}{8}$

7. $\frac{11}{13} - \frac{9}{13}$

8. $\frac{2}{3} - \frac{5}{9}$

9. $\frac{4}{5} - \frac{2}{3}$

10. $\frac{7}{12} + \frac{1}{3}$

11. $\frac{2}{3} + \frac{1}{4}$

12. $\frac{4}{5} + \frac{1}{10}$

Comparing Fractions

To compare fractions, determine which figure has more area shaded. If necessary, find equivalent fractions and compare the numerators.

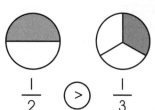

$$\frac{1}{2} \bigcirc{>} \frac{1}{3}$$

$$\frac{1}{2} = \frac{3}{6}$$

$$\frac{1}{3} = \frac{2}{6}$$

$$\frac{3}{6} \bigcirc{>} \frac{2}{6}$$

Write a fraction for the shaded area of each figure. Then, write >, <, or = to compare each pair of fractions.

1.

___ ___

2.

___ ___

3.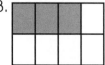

___ ___

4.

___ ___

5.

___ ___

6.

___ ___

Name: _____ Date: _____

Comparing Fractions

To compare fractions, find the equivalent fractions and compare the numerators.

Example: $\frac{1}{4}$ ◯ $\frac{1}{8}$ $\frac{1}{4} = \frac{2}{8}$

$\frac{1}{8} = \frac{1}{8}$ $\frac{2}{8}$ ⊙> $\frac{1}{8}$ $\frac{1}{4}$ ⊙> $\frac{1}{8}$

Write >, <, or = to compare each pair of fractions.

1. $\frac{5}{10}$ ◯ $\frac{2}{5}$ 2. $\frac{1}{6}$ ◯ $\frac{2}{3}$ 3. $\frac{5}{8}$ ◯ $\frac{6}{16}$

4. $\frac{5}{10}$ ◯ $\frac{1}{2}$ 5. $\frac{1}{12}$ ◯ $\frac{3}{8}$ 6. $\frac{6}{7}$ ◯ $\frac{3}{21}$

7. $\frac{4}{7}$ ◯ $\frac{8}{14}$ 8. $\frac{5}{12}$ ◯ $\frac{3}{4}$ 9. $\frac{4}{6}$ ◯ $\frac{7}{8}$

10. $\frac{1}{7}$ ◯ $\frac{4}{21}$ 11. $\frac{3}{8}$ ◯ $\frac{1}{2}$ 12. $\frac{3}{6}$ ◯ $\frac{1}{18}$

13. $\frac{1}{2}$ ◯ $\frac{3}{4}$ 14. $\frac{1}{6}$ ◯ $\frac{2}{12}$ 15. $\frac{3}{5}$ ◯ $\frac{1}{15}$

Comparing Fractions

To compare fractions, find the equivalent fractions and compare the numerators.

Example:

$$\frac{1}{4} \bigcirc \frac{1}{8} \qquad \frac{1}{4} = \frac{2}{8}$$

$$\frac{1}{8} = \frac{1}{8} \qquad \frac{2}{8} \enspace \text{\textcircled{>}} \enspace \frac{1}{8} \qquad \frac{1}{4} \enspace \text{\textcircled{>}} \enspace \frac{1}{8}$$

Write >, <, or = to compare each pair of fractions.

1. $\frac{1}{14} \bigcirc \frac{6}{7}$ 2. $\frac{3}{10} \bigcirc \frac{2}{5}$ 3. $\frac{1}{2} \bigcirc \frac{3}{4}$

4. $\frac{1}{6} \bigcirc \frac{2}{3}$ 5. $\frac{12}{20} \bigcirc \frac{6}{10}$ 6. $\frac{3}{7} \bigcirc \frac{2}{4}$

7. $\frac{3}{5} \bigcirc \frac{1}{2}$ 8. $\frac{1}{3} \bigcirc \frac{4}{9}$ 9. $\frac{8}{9} \bigcirc \frac{3}{5}$

10. $\frac{2}{3} \bigcirc \frac{7}{9}$ 11. $\frac{1}{3} \bigcirc \frac{2}{5}$ 12. $\frac{5}{8} \bigcirc \frac{15}{24}$

13. $\frac{6}{7} \bigcirc \frac{1}{3}$ 14. $\frac{1}{8} \bigcirc \frac{3}{4}$ 15. $\frac{4}{6} \bigcirc \frac{3}{8}$

16. $\frac{1}{3} \bigcirc \frac{5}{7}$ 17. $\frac{5}{8} \bigcirc \frac{2}{3}$ 18. $\frac{4}{5} \bigcirc \frac{1}{4}$

Mixed Numbers

When a numerator is greater than a denominator, the fraction is called an **improper fraction**. An improper fraction can be written as a **mixed number**, a whole number with a fraction. To change improper fractions into mixed numbers, follow these steps:

1. Divide the numerator by the denominator. The whole number in the quotient tells how many whole parts there are.

$$\frac{11}{5} \qquad 5)\overline{\begin{array}{r} 2 \\ 11 \\ -10 \\ \hline 1 \end{array}}$$

2. The remainder becomes the numerator, and the divisor becomes the denominator.

$$5)\overline{\begin{array}{r} 2\,R\,1 \\ 11 \\ -10 \\ \hline 1 \end{array}} = 2\frac{1}{5}$$

Change each improper fraction into a mixed number in lowest terms.

1. $\dfrac{15}{7} =$

2. $\dfrac{14}{4} =$

3. $\dfrac{7}{3} =$

4. $\dfrac{11}{5} =$

5. $\dfrac{17}{9} =$

6. $\dfrac{13}{4} =$

7. $\dfrac{16}{5} =$

8. $\dfrac{11}{2} =$

9. $\dfrac{10}{4} =$

10. $\dfrac{21}{5} =$

11. $\dfrac{23}{6} =$

12. $\dfrac{19}{6} =$

13. $\dfrac{9}{2} =$

14. $\dfrac{15}{6} =$

15. $\dfrac{26}{6} =$

16. $\dfrac{18}{8} =$

Mixed Numbers

To add mixed numbers, follow these steps:

1. Find the least common denominator and equivalent fractions if necessary.

$$3\frac{2}{3} \qquad \frac{2 \times 3}{3 \times 3} = \frac{6}{9}$$
$$+2\frac{7}{9} \qquad \frac{7 \times 1}{9 \times 1} = \frac{7}{9}$$

2. Add.

$$3\frac{6}{9}$$
$$+2\frac{7}{9}$$
$$\overline{\quad 5\frac{13}{9}}$$

3. Reduce and regroup if necessary.

$$3\frac{6}{9}$$
$$+2\frac{7}{9}$$
$$\overline{\quad 5\frac{13}{9} = 6\frac{4}{9}}$$

Add. Reduce sums to lowest terms.

1. $1\frac{1}{5}$
    $+3\frac{3}{5}$

2. $2\frac{4}{10}$
    $+7\frac{4}{10}$

3. $5\frac{4}{14}$
    $+4\frac{5}{14}$

4. $3\frac{3}{10}$
    $+3\frac{2}{10}$

5. $4\frac{2}{3}$
    $+6\frac{9}{12}$

6. $1\frac{3}{4}$
    $+1\frac{5}{8}$

7. $3\frac{6}{9}$
    $+5\frac{5}{9}$

8. $6\frac{2}{4}$
    $+\ \frac{8}{12}$

9. $6\frac{1}{2}$
    $+6\frac{9}{10}$

10. $1\frac{2}{3}$
    $+2\frac{5}{6}$

11. $3\frac{3}{5}$
    $+4\frac{8}{15}$

12. $3\frac{4}{6}$
    $+2\frac{5}{12}$

Mixed Numbers

To subtract mixed numbers, follow these steps:

1. Find the least common denominator and equivalent fractions if necessary.

2. Borrow and regroup if necessary. Subtract the fractions.

3. Subtract the whole numbers. Reduce to lowest terms if necessary.

$$5\frac{1}{8} \quad \frac{1 \times 3}{8 \times 3} = \frac{3}{24}$$
$$-2\frac{1}{3} \quad \frac{1 \times 8}{3 \times 8} = \frac{8}{24}$$

$$5\frac{3}{24}$$
$$-2\frac{8}{24}$$

$$\overset{4}{\cancel{5}}\,\overset{27}{\cancel{\frac{3}{24}}} \left(\frac{3}{24} + \frac{24}{24}\right)$$
$$-2\frac{8}{24}$$
$$\overline{\frac{19}{24}}$$

$$\overset{4}{\cancel{5}}\,\overset{27}{\cancel{\frac{3}{24}}}$$
$$-2\frac{8}{24}$$
$$\overline{2\frac{19}{24}}$$

Subtract. Reduce differences to lowest terms.

1. $6\frac{1}{4}$
   $-3\frac{5}{8}$

2. $9\frac{1}{5}$
   $-4\frac{6}{10}$

3. $2\frac{1}{10}$
   $-1\frac{4}{5}$

4. $9\frac{4}{7}$
   $-\frac{8}{14}$

5. $8\frac{5}{9}$
   $-2\frac{2}{3}$

6. $5\frac{1}{2}$
   $-\frac{3}{4}$

7. $6\frac{4}{9}$
   $-2\frac{3}{18}$

8. $10\frac{2}{3}$
   $-5\frac{18}{27}$

9. $7\frac{2}{5}$
   $-3\frac{1}{2}$

10. $10\frac{1}{2}$
    $-8\frac{6}{7}$

11. $7\frac{1}{3}$
    $-3\frac{4}{12}$

12. $6\frac{1}{3}$
    $-4\frac{3}{4}$

Decimals: Tenths

A **tenth** is the first digit after the decimal point. It is one part of 10. To find a tenth, count the number of boxes out of 10 that are shaded.

Example:  = 5.2 or five and two tenths

Write the decimal.

1.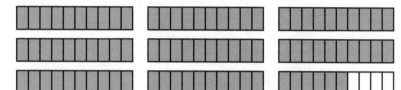

_____

2.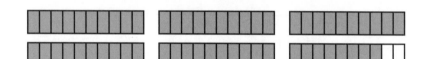

_____

3.

_____

4.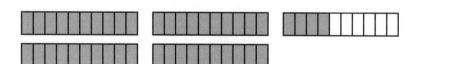

_____

Draw a line to match each number to its number word.

5. 3.7   seven and two tenths

6. 4.3   eight and nine tenths

7. 7.2   four and three tenths

8. 8.9   two and one tenth

9. 2.1   three and seven tenths

Decimals: Tenths

A **tenth** is the first digit after the decimal point. It is one part of 10. To find a tenth, count the number of boxes out of 10 that are shaded.

Example: Find the number of tenths in the box.

Six tenths of the box is shaded.

When there are no whole numbers, place a 0 before the decimal point.

The total can be written 0.6, $\frac{6}{10}$, or $\frac{3}{5}$

Find the number of tenths in each box. Write the total as a fraction in lowest terms and as a decimal.

1.

Fraction: _____

Decimal: _____

2.

Fraction: _____

Decimal: _____

3.

Fraction: _____

Decimal: _____

4.

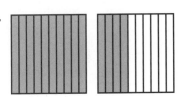

Fraction: _____

Decimal: _____

5.

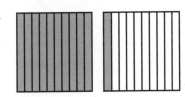

Fraction: _____

Decimal: _____

6.

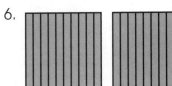

Fraction: _____

Decimal: _____

Name: _____ Date: _____

Decimals: Tenths

To write decimals in word form, write the word "and" as the decimal point.
Example: nine and seven tenths = 9.7 = $9\frac{7}{10}$

Write the decimal equivalent.

1. three and five tenths _____
2. six and one tenth _____
3. eight tenths _____
4. eight and three tenths _____
5. three tenths _____
6. two and one tenth _____
7. seven tenths _____
8. twenty and two tenths _____
9. four tenths _____
10. seven and two tenths _____

Write the number word for each decimal.

11. 3.9 _____
12. 2.7 _____
13. 12.8 _____
14. 7.3 _____
15. 0.5 _____
16. 1.1 _____
17. 6.4 _____
18. 2.6 _____
19. 4.2 _____
20. 4.4 _____

Write the fraction or mixed number in lowest terms that is equal to each decimal.

21. 0.6 _____
22. 0.5 _____
23. 0.9 _____
24. 0.7 _____
25. 1.2 _____
26. 4.8 _____

● ● ●

Decimals: Hundredths

A **hundredth** is the second digit after the decimal point. It is one part of 100. To find a hundredth, count the number of boxes out of 100 that are shaded.

Example:     =   1.37 or
one and thirty-seven hundredths

Write the decimal.

1. 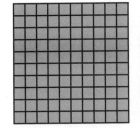  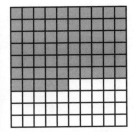   _____

2. 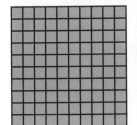 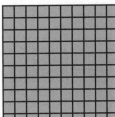 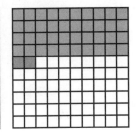   _____

Draw a line to match each number to its number word.

3. 4.31   forty-three hundredths

4. 7.26   eight and nine hundredths

5. 8.09   four and thirty-one hundredths

6. 0.43   seven and twenty-six hundredths

7. 6.73   six and seventy-three hundredths

Name: _____ Date: _____

Decimals: Hundredths

A **hundredth** is the second digit after the decimal point. It is one part of 100. To find a hundredth, count the number of boxes out of 100 that are shaded.

Example: Find the number of hundredths in the box.

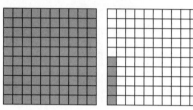

One whole box is shaded and
five hundredths of the second box is shaded.

The total can be written 1.05, $1\frac{5}{100}$, or $1\frac{1}{20}$

Find the number of hundredths in each box. Write the total as a fraction in lowest terms and as a decimal.

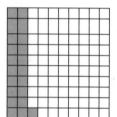   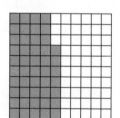   

1. Fraction: _____   2. Fraction: _____   3. Fraction: _____

   Decimal: _____   Decimal: _____   Decimal: _____

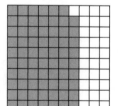   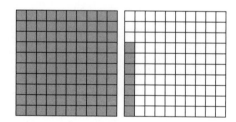   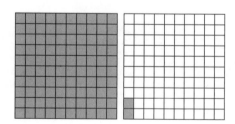

4. Fraction: _____   5. Fraction: _____   6. Fraction: _____

   Decimal: _____   Decimal: _____   Decimal: _____

● ● **Step Up to Math** · **Intermediate** · **CD-104260** · © **Carson-Dellosa**

Decimals: Hundredths

To write decimals in word form, write the word "and" as the decimal point.

Example: twenty-six and forty-two hundredths = 26.42 = $26\frac{42}{100}$ = $26\frac{21}{50}$

Write the decimal equivalent.

1. nine and sixteen hundredths _____

2. fourteen and seventy-two hundredths _____

3. two hundred and thirty-four hundredths _____

4. forty-seven and eighty-nine hundredths _____

5. eleven and sixty-two hundredths _____

Write the equivalent fraction or mixed number of each decimal in lowest terms.

6. 0.08 _____   7. 6.09 _____   8. 2.12 _____

9. 0.21 _____   10. 7.34 _____   11. 0.55 _____

12. 16.08 _____   13. 300.24 _____   14. 25.04 _____

15. 600.49 _____   16. 0.72 _____   17. 0.22 _____

18. 25.34 _____   19. 9.09 _____   20. 4.39 _____

Decimals: Thousandths

A **thousandth** is the third digit to the right of the decimal point. It is one part of 1,000.

Example: In the number 0.432, the 2 is in the thousandths place.
The decimal is written as four hundred thirty-two thousandths.

Underline each digit in the thousandths place.

1. 0.346	2. 3.254	3. 0.034
4. 4.100	5. 0.295	6. 6.521
7. 0.593	8. 5.042	9. 12.105
10. 6.003	11. 2.049	12. 3.512

Draw a line to match each number word to its decimal equivalent.

13.	two hundred forty-one thousandths	0.150
14.	four thousandths	0.922
15.	one hundred fifty thousandths	0.004
16.	nine hundred twenty-two thousandths	0.241
17.	eight hundred fifteen thousandths	0.100
18.	five thousandths	0.815
19.	three hundred fifty-one thousandths	0.005
20.	one hundred thousandths	0.351

Decimals: Thousandths

A **thousandth** is the third digit to the right of the decimal point. It is one part of 1,000.

Example: four hundred thirty-two thousandths = 0.432

Draw a line to match each number word to its decimal equivalent.

1.	four hundred twenty-five thousandths	0.126
2.	one hundred twenty-six thousandths	0.900
3.	nine hundred thousandths	0.649
4.	seven hundred seventy-eight thousandths	0.002
5.	two hundred thirty-six thousandths	0.425
6.	six hundred forty-nine thousandths	0.518
7.	five hundred eighteen thousandths	0.586
8.	two thousandths	0.927
9.	five hundred eighty-six thousandths	0.778
10.	nine hundred twenty-seven thousandths	0.236

Write the correct number words for each decimal.

11. 0.934 _____ hundred _____ - _____ thousandths

12. 0.200 _____ hundred thousandths

13. 0.350 _____ hundred _____ thousandths

14. 0.925 _____ hundred _____ - _____ thousandths

15. 0.194 _____ hundred _____ - _____ thousandths

16. 0.973 _____ hundred _____ - _____ thousandths

17. 0.429 _____ hundred _____ - _____ thousandths

18. 0.486 _____ hundred _____ - _____ thousandths

19. 0.971 _____ hundred _____ - _____ thousandths

20. 0.052 _____ - _____ thousandths

Name: _____   Date: _____

Decimals: Thousandths

A **thousandth** is the third digit to the right of the decimal point. It is one part of 1,000. To write decimals in word form, write the word "and" as the decimal point.

Example: twenty-five and two hundred seventeen thousandths = 25.217 = $25\frac{217}{1,000}$

Write the decimal equivalent.

1.   three hundred seven thousandths   _____

2.   fifteen and forty-five thousandths   _____

3.   two hundred eighteen thousandths   _____

4.   two thousandths   _____

Write the number word for each decimal.

5.   0.035 _____

_____

6.   89.004 _____

_____

7.   18.427 _____

_____

Write the equivalent fraction or mixed number of each decimal.

8.   0.237 _____   9.   6.259 _____   10.   2.633 _____

11.   0.651 _____   12.   7.529 _____   13.   0.981 _____

14.   1.253 _____   15.   8.779 _____   16.   0.437 _____

Comparing and Ordering Decimals

To order decimals with whole numbers, treat the whole numbers like decimals. For example, whole numbers would be written 1.0, 2.0, and 3.0. Then, order the numbers. On the number lines below, each mark represents one tenth.

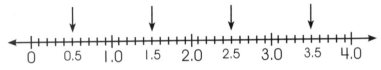

Write the missing decimals.

1.

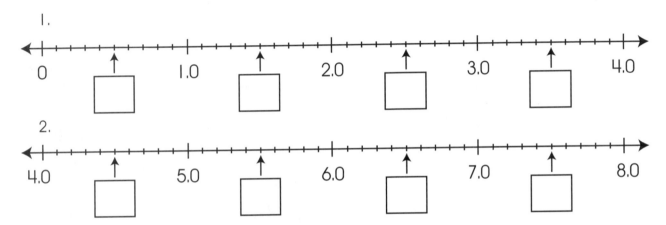

2.

Write the numbers in order from least to greatest.

3. | 2.0 0.5 1.0 1.5 |

4. | 2.5 1.5 2.0 3.0 |

5. | 3.0 3.5 2.5 0.5 |
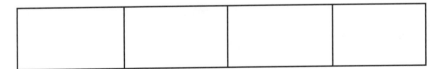

6. | 3.5 2.5 5.5 4.5 4.0 |

Comparing and Ordering Decimals

To compare decimals, follow these steps:

1. Look at the number of digits to the left of the decimal point. Are they the same? If not, the number with the most digits is greater.

2. If the number of digits is the same, begin with the first digit on the left. Which number has a larger digit? That is the greater number.

3. If the digits are the same, move to the next place value and find the larger digit.

4. Continue from left to right until you find a digit in the same place value with a greater value.

Example: 0.4 ⟨>⟩ 0.2   0.13 ⟨<⟩ 0.34

Write > or < to compare each pair of decimals.

1. 0.6 ◯ 0.4   2. 0.1 ◯ 0.5   3. 0.23 ◯ 0.03

4. 0.6 ◯ 0.9   5. 0.06 ◯ 0.60   6. 0.4 ◯ 0.7

7. 0.9 ◯ 0.5   8. 0.7 ◯ 0.6   9. 0.42 ◯ 0.14

10. 0.72 ◯ 0.27   11. 0.25 ◯ 0.52   12. 0.7 ◯ 0.3

13. 1.4 ◯ 1.6   14. 3.5 ◯ 3.7   15. 16.2 ◯ 16.8

Comparing and Ordering Decimals

To compare decimals, follow these steps:

1. Look at the number of digits to the left of the decimal point. Are they the same? If not, the number with the most digits is greater.

2. If the number of digits is the same, begin with the first digit on the left. Which number has a larger digit? That is the greater number.

3. If the digits are the same, move to the next place value and find the larger digit.

4. Continue from left to right until you find a digit in the same place value with a greater value.

Write >, <, or = to compare each pair of decimals.

1. 3.4 ◯ 4.5

2. 6.01 ◯ 2.06

3. 5.01 ◯ 5.09

4. 3.02 ◯ 2.03

5. 0.567 ◯ 0.563

6. 56.001 ◯ 56.01

7. 3.003 ◯ 3.003

8. 5.9 ◯ 5.09

9. 6.01 ◯ 2.06

10. 1.456 ◯ 1.665

11. 8.076 ◯ 8.076

12. 2.798 ◯ 2.709

13. 11.587 ◯ 11.586

14. 56.02 ◯ 56.20

15. 0.845 ◯ 1.085

16. 5.025 ◯ 5.018

17. 3.772 ◯ 3.225

18. 3.187 ◯ 3.948

Rounding Decimals

To round a decimal, follow these steps:

1. Underline the place value you are rounding to.

2. If the number to the right of the underline is 0, 1, 2, 3, or 4, the underlined digit stays the same.

3. If the number to the right of the underline is 5, 6, 7, 8, or 9, the underlined digit goes up by 1.

Examples: Round to the nearest whole number: $\underline{4}.8$ rounds up to 5

Round to the nearest dollar: $\$14.\underline{2}4$ rounds down to $\$14.00$

Round to the nearest whole number.

1. 6.2 _____   2. 24.7 _____   3. 3.5 _____

4. 3.4 _____   5. 10.3 _____   6. 9.4 _____

7. 5.4 _____   8. 112.6 _____   9. 6.8 _____

10. 17.6 _____   11. 14.8 _____   12. 28.5 _____

Round to the nearest dollar.

13. $3.67 _____   14. $10.51 _____   15. $9.21 _____

16. $21.24 _____   17. $7.82 _____   18. $8.30 _____

19. $8.67 _____   20. $10.38 _____   21. $5.93 _____

22. $9.79 _____   23. $11.24 _____   24. $14.27 _____

Name: _____   Date: _____   85

Rounding Decimals

To round a decimal, follow these steps:

1. Underline the place value you are rounding to.

2. If the number to the right of the underline is 0, 1, 2, 3, or 4, the underlined digit stays the same.

3. If the number to the right of the underline is 5, 6, 7, 8, or 9, the underlined digit goes up by 1.

Examples: Round to the nearest tenth: 23.8<u>6</u> rounds up to 23.9

Round to the nearest dollar: $26.3<u>4</u> rounds down to $26.00

Round each number to the nearest whole number.

1. 45.6 _____   2. 2.6 _____

3. 612.1 _____   4. 345.5 _____

5. 7.2 _____   6. 1.3 _____

7. 87.5 _____   8. 43.9 _____

Round each number to the nearest tenth.

9. 4.37 _____   10. 2.89 _____

11. 543.18 _____   12. 56.14 _____

13. 3.15 _____   14. 78.08 _____

15. 0.41 _____   16. 36.19 _____

Round each number to the nearest dollar.

17. $34.64 _____   18. $25.55 _____

19. $64.10 _____   20. $23.21 _____

21. $39.17 _____   22. $23.68 _____

23. $12.85 _____   24. $29.01 _____

Rounding Decimals

To round a decimal, follow these steps:

1. Underline the place value you are rounding to.

2. If the number to the right of the underline is 0, 1, 2, 3, or 4, the underlined digit stays the same.

3. If the number to the right of the underline is 5, 6, 7, 8, or 9, the underlined digit goes up by 1.

Examples: Round to the nearest tenth: 48.6$\underline{7}$ rounds up to 48.7

Round to the nearest hundredth: 315.46$\underline{2}$ rounds down to 315.46

Round each number to the nearest whole number.

1. 15.3 _____   2. 3.6 _____

3. 57.1 _____   4. 722.5 _____

5. 37.8 _____   6. 623.9 _____

7. 18.9 _____   8. 78.4 _____

Round each number to the nearest tenth.

9. 56.32 _____   10. 10.85 _____

11. 41.12 _____   12. 132.75 _____

13. 18.76 _____   14. 5.39 _____

15. 307.68 _____   16. 60.36 _____

Round each number to the nearest hundredth.

17. 230.036 _____   18. 0.296 _____

19. 155.872 _____   20. 59.305 _____

21. 35.512 _____   22. 158.335 _____

23. 725.977 _____   24. 82.361 _____

Adding Decimals

To add decimals, follow these steps:

1. Line up the decimal points. Bring down the decimal point to the answer.

2. Add the lowest place value column.

3. Add the next place value column.

4. Add the next place value column if necessary.

4.23	4.23	4.23	4.23
+ 5.55	+ 5.55	+ 5.55	+ 5.55
.	. 8	.78	9.78

Add.

1.   2.1
    + 2.1

2.   6.4
    + 3.2

3.   3.1
    + 1.2

4.   3.2
    + 5.0

5.   3.13
    + 1.01

6.   9.52
    + 0.25

7.   8.02
    + 1.43

8.   7.1
    + 1.1

9.   6.6
    + 2.2

10.   2.4
    + 5.3

11.   7.30
    + 2.20

12.   6.03
    + 1.81

13.   2.31
    + 0.23

14.   4.61
    + 3.21

15.   4.0
    + 5.1

16.   4.2
    + 3.4

Adding Decimals

To add decimals, follow these steps:

1. Line up the decimal points. Bring down the decimal point to the answer.

2. Add the numbers in the lowest place value column. Regroup if necessary.

3. Add the numbers in the next place value column. Regroup if necessary.

4. Add the numbers in the ones and tens places. Regroup if necessary.

```
   24.63          24.63          24.63          24.63
 +  4.55        +  4.55        +  4.55        +  4.55
     .              . 8           .18          29.18
```

Add.

1. 17.21
 + 8.42

2. 27.4
 + 13.1

3. 31.9
 + 20.8

4. 57.6
 + 31.9

5. 53.41
 + 41.23

6. 65.6
 + 22.4

7. 7.92
 + 0.42

8. 41.32
 + 4.95

9. 11.24
 + 8.09

10. 60.42
  + 8.19

11. 23.64
  + 31.95

12. 43.04
  + 21.89

13. 63.57
  + 10.92

14. 7.42
  + 5.49

15. 52.81
  + 15.92

Adding Decimals

To add decimals, follow these steps:
1. Line up the decimal points.
2. Bring down the decimal point to the answer.
3. Add the lowest place value column. Regroup if necessary.
4. Add the next place value column. Regroup if necessary.
5. Add the next place value column. Regroup if necessary.
6. Add the next place value column if necessary.

Add.

1. $3.20 + 21.14 + 321.90$

2. $0.340 + 0.200 + 0.121$

3. $7.000 + 0.340 + 1.215$

4. $23.700 + 0.416$

5. $49.10 + 0.84 + 1.30$

6. $14.600 + 0.300 + 1.257$

Add.

7.
```
    6.00
    3.20
+   0.45
```

8.
```
    3.145
    0.200
+  15.900
```

9.
```
    8.462
+  23.890
```

10.
```
    7.000
    6.430
+  12.125
```

11.
```
   24.500
    0.900
+   1.238
```

12.
```
    0.60
   12.30
+   0.14
```

13.
```
   76.400
    3.516
+   3.140
```

14.
```
    0.814
   21.300
+   3.140
```

Name: _____   Date: _____

Subtracting Decimals

To subtract decimals, follow these steps:

1. Line up the decimal points. Bring down the decimal point to the answer.

2. Subtract the lowest place value column.

3. Subtract the next place value column.

4. Subtract the next place value column if necessary.

```
    4.75          4.75          4.75          4.75
  - 2.23        - 2.23        - 2.23        - 2.23
       .           .  2          .52          2.52
```

Subtract.

1.
```
   2.8
 - 0.2
```

2.
```
   6.9
 - 3.1
```

3.
```
   3.96
 - 1.22
```

4.
```
   5.6
 - 2.6
```

5.
```
   3.59
 - 0.41
```

6.
```
   9.59
 - 0.18
```

7.
```
   8.57
 - 2.36
```

8.
```
   7.7
 - 1.3
```

9.
```
   6.8
 - 5.3
```

10.
```
   5.9
 - 1.8
```

11.
```
   7.29
 - 2.11
```

12.
```
   5.63
 - 1.41
```

13.
```
   2.38
 - 0.16
```

14.
```
   4.99
 - 2.83
```

15.
```
   9.9
 - 1.2
```

Subtracting Decimals

To subtract decimals, follow these steps:

1. Line up the decimal points. Bring down the decimal point to the answer.	2. Subtract the lowest place value column. Regroup if necessary.	3. Subtract the next place value column. Regroup if necessary.	4. Subtract the ones and tens. Regroup if necessary.
$\begin{array}{r} 24.73 \\ -\ 12.55 \\ \hline \ \ \ \ \ . \end{array}$	$\begin{array}{r} {}^{6\ 13} \\ 24.\cancel{73} \\ -\ 12.55 \\ \hline .\ 8 \end{array}$	$\begin{array}{r} {}^{6\ 13} \\ 24.\cancel{73} \\ -\ 12.55 \\ \hline .18 \end{array}$	$\begin{array}{r} {}^{6\ 13} \\ 24.\cancel{73} \\ -\ 12.55 \\ \hline 12.18 \end{array}$

Subtract.

1. $\begin{array}{r} 14.6 \\ -\ 2.9 \end{array}$	2. $\begin{array}{r} 1.63 \\ -\ 0.20 \end{array}$	3. $\begin{array}{r} 36.85 \\ -\ 22.93 \end{array}$	4. $\begin{array}{r} 19.98 \\ -\ 11.30 \end{array}$	5. $\begin{array}{r} 30.4 \\ -\ 8.2 \end{array}$
6. $\begin{array}{r} 6.27 \\ -\ 3.14 \end{array}$	7. $\begin{array}{r} 45.84 \\ -\ 11.38 \end{array}$	8. $\begin{array}{r} 56.52 \\ -\ 33.19 \end{array}$	9. $\begin{array}{r} 43.6 \\ -\ 21.5 \end{array}$	10. $\begin{array}{r} 22.68 \\ -\ 1.39 \end{array}$
11. $\begin{array}{r} 3.42 \\ -\ 1.81 \end{array}$	12. $\begin{array}{r} 43.95 \\ -\ 17.28 \end{array}$	13. $\begin{array}{r} 29.34 \\ -\ 28.22 \end{array}$	14. $\begin{array}{r} 11.7 \\ -\ 8.4 \end{array}$	15. $\begin{array}{r} 69.42 \\ -\ 57.09 \end{array}$
16. $\begin{array}{r} 99.38 \\ -\ 81.46 \end{array}$	17. $\begin{array}{r} 54.29 \\ -\ 13.82 \end{array}$	18. $\begin{array}{r} 45.49 \\ -\ 41.79 \end{array}$	19. $\begin{array}{r} 23.49 \\ -\ 19.82 \end{array}$	20. $\begin{array}{r} 13.22 \\ -\ 12.03 \end{array}$

Name: _____ Date: _____

Subtracting Decimals

To subtract decimals, follow these steps:
1. Line up the decimal points.
2. Bring down the decimal point to the answer.
3. Subtract the lowest place value column. Regroup if necessary.
4. Subtract the next place value column. Regroup if necessary.
5. Subtract the next place value column. Regroup if necessary.
6. Subtract the next place value column.

Subtract.

1. $\begin{array}{r} 48.120 \\ -\ 22.059 \\ \hline \end{array}$

2. $\begin{array}{r} 46.300 \\ -\ 23.024 \\ \hline \end{array}$

3. $\begin{array}{r} 15.876 \\ -\ 2.329 \\ \hline \end{array}$

4. $\begin{array}{r} 35.960 \\ -\ 17.328 \\ \hline \end{array}$

5. $\begin{array}{r} 35.402 \\ -\ 21.280 \\ \hline \end{array}$

6. $\begin{array}{r} 17.64 \\ -\ 2.84 \\ \hline \end{array}$

7. $\begin{array}{r} 68.40 \\ -\ 32.32 \\ \hline \end{array}$

8. $\begin{array}{r} 12.085 \\ -\ 10.658 \\ \hline \end{array}$

9. $\begin{array}{r} 65.603 \\ -\ 40.318 \\ \hline \end{array}$

10. $\begin{array}{r} 45.50 \\ -\ 12.36 \\ \hline \end{array}$

11. $\begin{array}{r} 3.00 \\ -\ 1.34 \\ \hline \end{array}$

12. $\begin{array}{r} 65.060 \\ -\ 21.325 \\ \hline \end{array}$

13. $\begin{array}{r} 43.460 \\ -\ 32.126 \\ \hline \end{array}$

14. $\begin{array}{r} 63.450 \\ -\ 51.232 \\ \hline \end{array}$

15. $\begin{array}{r} 64.800 \\ -\ 32.317 \\ \hline \end{array}$

16. $\begin{array}{r} 77.600 \\ -\ 65.135 \\ \hline \end{array}$

17. $\begin{array}{r} 33.803 \\ -\ 21.999 \\ \hline \end{array}$

18. $\begin{array}{r} 89.429 \\ -\ 63.560 \\ \hline \end{array}$

19. $\begin{array}{r} 34.437 \\ -\ 12.239 \\ \hline \end{array}$

20. $\begin{array}{r} 6.022 \\ -\ 3.655 \\ \hline \end{array}$

Name: _____ Date: _____ 93

Multiplying Money

To multiply money, follow these steps:

1. Multiply the top number by the second number. Regroup if necessary.
2. Count the number of places after the decimal point. When multiplying money, there are two places after the decimal point. Write a decimal point in the product two places from the right.
3. Write the dollar sign.

$$
\begin{array}{r}
\$5.00 \\
\times\quad 8 \\
\hline
\$40.00
\end{array}
$$

Multiply. Remember to include the dollar sign and the decimal point.

1. $7.00
    x   5

2. $4.00
    x   8

3. $8.00
    x   3

4. $6.00
    x   7

5. $9.00
    x   2

6. $1.00
    x   4

7. $3.00
    x   6

8. $2.00
    x   5

9. $1.00
    x   7

10. $7.00
    x   9

11. $4.00
    x   6

12. $3.00
    x   9

13. $6.00
    x   8

14. $3.00
    x   3

15. $4.00
    x   4

16. $7.00
    x   6

Name: _____   Date: _____

Multiplying Money

To multiply money, follow these steps:

1. Multiply the top number by the ones digit in the second number. Regroup if necessary.

2. Write a zero in the ones column.

3. Multiply the top number by the tens digit in the second number if necessary. Regroup if necessary.

4. Add. Regroup if necessary. Write a decimal point two places from the right. Write a dollar sign.

```
    1              2              2              2
  $3.51          $3.51          $3.51          $3.51
x   42         x   42         x   42         x   42
  702            702            702            702
                   0          14040         + 14040
                                             $147.42
```

Multiply. Remember to include the dollar sign and the decimal point.

1.
```
  $2.41
x     3
```

2.
```
  $3.89
x     6
```

3.
```
  $0.21
x     4
```

4.
```
  $24.12
x      8
```

5.
```
  $0.84
x     3
```

6.
```
  $15.41
x      3
```

7.
```
  $4.21
x     7
```

8.
```
  $0.74
x     5
```

9.
```
  $0.49
x    21
```

10.
```
  $9.25
x    34
```

11.
```
  $3.24
x    14
```

12.
```
  $8.54
x    16
```

13.
```
  $2.12
x    42
```

14.
```
  $0.13
x    92
```

15.
```
  $7.54
x    85
```

16.
```
  $3.38
x    65
```

Multiplying Money

To multiply money, follow these steps:

1. Multiply the top number by the ones digit in the second number. Regroup if necessary.

2. Write a zero in the ones column.

3. Multiply the top number by the tens digit in the second number. Regroup if necessary.

4. Add. Regroup if necessary. Write a decimal point two places from the right. Write a dollar sign.

```
      1                  2                   2                   2
    $3.51              $3.51               $3.51               $3.51
  x    42            x    42             x    42             x    42
    7 02               7 02                7 02                7 02
                          0              140 40             + 140 40
                                                            $147.42
```

Multiply. Remember to include the dollar sign and the decimal point.

1.	$4.89 x 16	2.	$51.06 x 28	3.	$49.22 x 43	4.	$82.56 x 27
5.	$5.89 x 54	6.	$3.99 x 35	7.	$8.41 x 32	8.	$3.53 x 64
9.	$41.25 x 39	10.	$8.86 x 74	11.	$0.98 x 48	12.	$0.59 x 76
13.	$4.86 x 27	14.	$38.48 x 19	15.	$8.58 x 23	16.	$46.92 x 17

Dividing Money

To divide money, follow these steps:

1. Write the dollar sign and the decimal point in the quotient.

$$\begin{array}{r} \$. \\ 4\overline{)\$8.00} \end{array}$$

2. Divide into the ones place. Multiply the divisor by this quotient. Write the product under the ones digit. Subtract.

$$\begin{array}{r} \$2. \\ 4\overline{)\$8.00} \\ -\ 8 \\ \hline 0 \end{array}$$

3. Bring down the 0. Try to divide. Subtract. Bring down the 0.

$$\begin{array}{r} \$2.0 \\ 4\overline{)\$8.00} \\ -\ 8 \\ \hline 0\,0 \\ -\ 0 \\ \hline 00 \end{array}$$

4. Try to divide. Subtract.

$$\begin{array}{r} \$2.00 \\ 4\overline{)\$8.00} \\ -\ 8 \\ \hline 0\,0 \\ -\ 0 \\ \hline 00 \\ -\ 0 \\ \hline 0 \end{array}$$

Divide. Remember to include the dollar sign and the decimal point.

1. $2\overline{)\$4.00}$ 2. $3\overline{)\$9.00}$ 3. $3\overline{)\$6.00}$

4. $2\overline{)\$6.00}$ 5. $5\overline{)\$5.00}$ 6. $4\overline{)\$12.00}$

7. $3\overline{)\$15.00}$ 8. $2\overline{)\$10.00}$ 9. $6\overline{)\$6.00}$

Name: _____ Date: _____

Dividing Money

To divide money, follow these steps:

1. Write the dollar sign and the decimal point in the quotient.

$$3\overline{)\$6.48} \quad \$\,.$$

2. Divide into the ones place. Multiply the divisor by this quotient. Subtract.

$$\begin{array}{r} \$2. \\ 3\overline{)\$6.48} \\ -6 \\ \hline 0 \end{array}$$

3. Bring down the next digit. Divide the divisor into this number. Subtract.

$$\begin{array}{r} \$2.1 \\ 3\overline{)\$6.48} \\ -6 \\ \hline 04 \\ -3 \\ \hline 1 \end{array}$$

4. Bring down the next digit. Divide the divisor into this number. Subtract.

$$\begin{array}{r} \$2.16 \\ 3\overline{)\$6.48} \\ -6 \\ \hline 04 \\ -3 \\ \hline 18 \\ -18 \\ \hline 0 \end{array}$$

Divide. Remember to include the dollar sign and the decimal point.

1. $2\overline{)\$6.48}$ 2. $3\overline{)\$6.69}$ 3. $5\overline{)\$6.35}$ 4. $8\overline{)\$9.12}$

5. $4\overline{)\$8.64}$ 6. $4\overline{)\$8.72}$ 7. $7\overline{)\$7.91}$ 8. $4\overline{)\$9.44}$

9. $6\overline{)\$6.48}$ 10. $7\overline{)\$8.68}$ 11. $4\overline{)\$8.76}$ 12. $5\overline{)\$9.20}$

Dividing Money

To divide money, follow these steps:

1. Write the dollar sign and the decimal point in the quotient.

$$\begin{array}{r} \$\ . \\ 3\overline{)\$12.75} \end{array}$$

2. Divide into the ones and tens places. Multiply the divisor by this quotient. Subtract.

$$\begin{array}{r} \$4. \\ 3\overline{)\$12.75} \\ -12 \\ \hline 0 \end{array}$$

3. Bring down the next digit. Divide the divisor into this number. Subtract.

$$\begin{array}{r} \$4.2 \\ 3\overline{)\$12.75} \\ -12 \\ \hline 07 \\ -6 \\ \hline 1 \end{array}$$

4. Bring down the next digit. Divide the divisor into this number. Subtract.

$$\begin{array}{r} \$4.25 \\ 3\overline{)\$12.75} \\ -12 \\ \hline 07 \\ -6 \\ \hline 15 \\ -15 \\ \hline 0 \end{array}$$

Divide. Remember to include the dollar sign and the decimal point.

1. $2\overline{)\$10.96}$

2. $3\overline{)\$2.34}$

3. $2\overline{)\$12.42}$

4. $5\overline{)\$17.95}$

5. $4\overline{)\$24.96}$

6. $8\overline{)\$8.40}$

7. $4\overline{)\$28.48}$

8. $6\overline{)\$22.74}$

9. $3\overline{)\$17.64}$

10. $7\overline{)\$13.09}$

11. $6\overline{)\$24.66}$

12. $3\overline{)\$10.68}$

13. $5\overline{)\$3.80}$

14. $4\overline{)\$15.56}$

15. $5\overline{)\$7.35}$

16. $5\overline{)\$31.05}$

Symmetry

A **line of symmetry** is a line that divides a figure into two matching parts. If a figure has one or more lines of symmetry, the figure is **symmetrical**. These figures are symmetrical:

 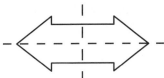

Circle the letter of the symmetrical figure in each row.

1. A. 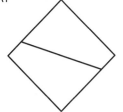   B.    C. 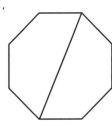   D.

2. A. 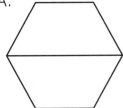   B.    C. 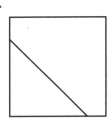   D.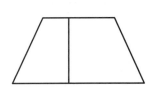

3. A. 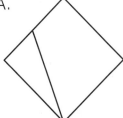   B.    C. 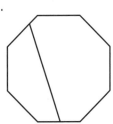   D.

4. A. 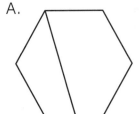   B. 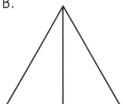   C. 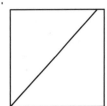   D.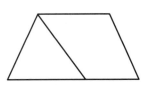

Name: _____   Date: _____

Symmetry

A **line of symmetry** is a line that divides a figure into two matching parts. If a figure has one or more lines of symmetry, the figure is **symmetrical**. These figures are symmetrical:

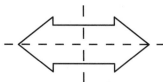

Draw a line of symmetry on each object.

1.

2.

3.

4.

5.

6.

Draw two lines of symmetry on each figure.

7.

8.

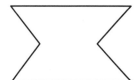

9.

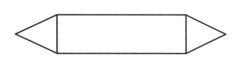

Name: _____ Date: _____

Symmetry

A **line of symmetry** is a line that divides a figure into two identical parts. If a figure has one or more lines of symmetry, the figure is **symmetrical**. Some figures have many lines of symmetry. These figures are symmetrical:

Is each figure symmetrical? Write *yes* or *no*.

1. 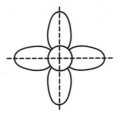   2.   3.   4. 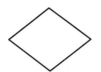   5.

_____ _____ _____ _____ _____

6.   7.   8.   9.   10.

_____ _____ _____ _____ _____

11. 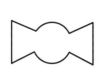   12.   13.   14.   15.

_____ _____ _____ _____ _____

Draw all of the lines of symmetry on each figure.

16.   17.    18.   19.    20.

Congruency

Figures that are the same shape but not the same size are **similar**. Figures that are the same size and shape are **congruent**.

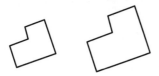

These figures are similar.

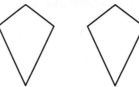

These figures are congruent.

Draw a line to connect each set of similar figures.

1.

2.

3.

4.

5.

Draw a line to connect each set of congruent figures.

6.

7.

8.

9.

10.

Name: _____   Date: _____

Congruency

Congruent figures are the same size and shape. They may look different because their positions can change. Congruent figures that slide, flip, or turn are still congruent. Figures that are the same shape but not the same size are **similar**.

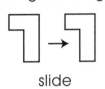 slide 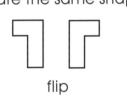 flip 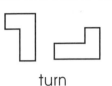 turn similar

Decide if each set of figures is congruent or similar. If they are congruent, write *slide*, *flip*, or *turn*. If they are similar, write *similar*.

1.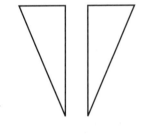

_____

2.

_____

3.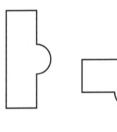

_____

4.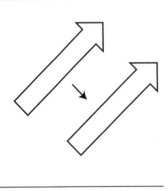

_____

5.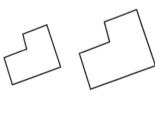

_____

6.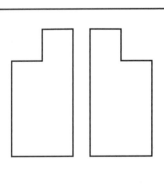

_____

Congruency

Figures that are the same shape but not the same size are **similar**. Figures that are the same size and shape are **congruent**.

These figures are similar.

These figures are congruent.

Draw a line to connect the figures that are similar.

1.

2.

Draw a line to connect the figures that are congruent.

3.

4.

Name: _____   Date: _____

Line Segments, Lines, and Rays

A **line segment** is a finite portion of a line that contains two endpoints. This figure is named line segment AB.

A **line** is a set of points in a straight path that extends infinitely in two directions. This figure is named line JK.

A **ray** is a portion of a line that extends from one endpoint infinitely in one direction. This figure is named ray ST.

A ———————— B   J ‹——————› K   S ——————› T

Identify each figure as a line segment, line, or ray.

1.

_____

2.

_____

3.

_____

4.

_____

5.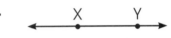

_____

6.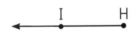

_____

Name each line segment, line, or ray.

7.

_____

8.

_____

9.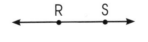

_____

10.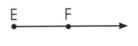

_____

11.

_____

12.

_____

Name: _____   Date: _____

Line Segments, Lines, and Rays

A **line segment** is a finite portion of a line that contains two endpoints. This figure is named $\overline{XY}$.

A **line** is a set of points in a straight path that extends infinitely in two directions. This figure is named $\overleftrightarrow{CD}$.

A **ray** is a portion of a line that extends from one endpoint infinitely in one direction. This figure is named $\overrightarrow{TX}$.

Lines that never cross are called **parallel lines**.

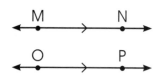

Lines that cross are called **intersecting lines**.

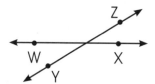

Lines that cross at right angles are called **perpendicular lines**.

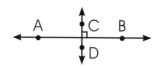

Name each figure.

1.

_____

2.

_____

3.

_____

4.

_____

5.

_____

6.

_____

7.

_____

8.

_____

9.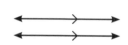

_____

Identify each figure as parallel lines, intersecting lines, or perpendicular lines.

10.

_____
_____

11.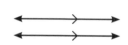

_____
_____

12.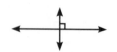

_____
_____

● ●

Name: _____ Date: _____

Line Segments, Lines, and Rays

A **line segment** is a finite portion of a line that contains two endpoints. This figure is named $\overline{AB}$.

A ●————————————● B

A **line** is a set of points in a straight path that extends infinitely in two directions. This figure is named $\overleftrightarrow{CD}$.

C ●————————————● D

A **ray** is a portion of a line that extends from one endpoint infinitely in one direction. This figure is named $\overrightarrow{MN}$.

M ●————————————● N

Lines that never cross are called **parallel lines**.

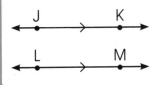

Lines that cross are called **intersecting lines**.

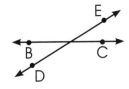

Lines that cross at right angles are called **perpendicular lines**.

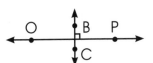

A flat surface that extends infinitely in all directions is called a **plane**. (plane D)

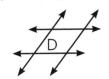

Name each figure.

1.  M   N

   _____

2.   S   T

   _____

3.   U   V

   _____

Identify each figure as parallel lines, intersecting lines, or perpendicular lines.

4.

   _____

   _____

5.

   _____

   _____

6.

   _____

   _____

Use the figure to the right to answer each statement. Write *True* or *False*.

7. _____ The figure is plane W.

8. _____ The "X" is made of rays.

9. _____ $\overleftrightarrow{JK}$ and $\overleftrightarrow{LM}$ are parallel.

10. _____ $\overrightarrow{EF}$ and $\overrightarrow{GH}$ intersect.

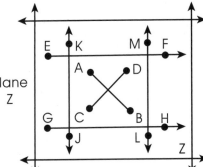

Plane Z

Name: _____   Date: _____

Angles

The point at which two rays meet to form an angle is called a **vertex**. Point N is the vertex.

An angle that is less than 90° is called an **acute** angle.

An angle that is 90° is called a **right** angle.

An angle greater than 90° is called an **obtuse** angle.

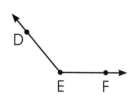

Identify each angle below as either acute, right, or obtuse.

1.
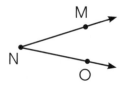
_____

2.
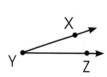
_____

3.

_____

4.
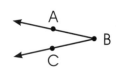
_____

5.
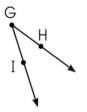
_____

6.

_____

7.
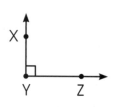
_____

8.
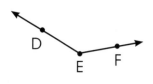
_____

9.

_____

Angles

The point at which two rays meet to form an angle is called a **vertex**. Point N is the vertex.

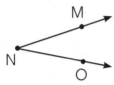

An angle that is less than 90° is called an **acute** angle.

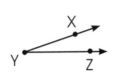

An angle that is 90° is called a **right** angle.

An angle greater than 90° is called an **obtuse** angle.

Identify each angle below as either acute, right, or obtuse.

1.
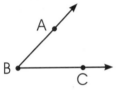

_____

2.
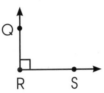

_____

3.
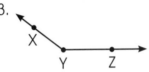

_____

4.
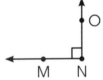

_____

5.
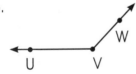

_____

6.
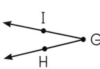

_____

7.
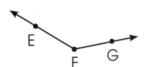

_____

8.

_____

9.
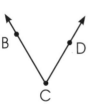

_____

10.
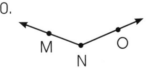

_____

11.
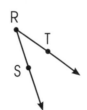

_____

12.
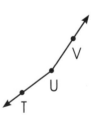

_____

Angles

A **protractor** measures the degree of an angle. To use a protractor, follow these steps:

1. Find the center dot or intersecting segments along the straight edge on the bottom of the protractor.

2. Place the dot or intersecting segments over the **vertex**, or point, of the angle you wish to measure.

3. Rotate the protractor so that the 0 mark on the straight edge lines up with one ray of the angle.

4. Find the point where the second ray of the angle intersects the numbered edge of the protractor. If the angle does not extend far enough to intersect the numbered edge, use the protractor as a straight edge to extend the angle line. Then, realign the protractor with the vertex and 0.

5. Read the number that is written on the protractor at the point where the ray intersects the protractor's edge. This is the measure of the angle in degrees.

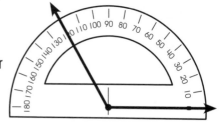

Use a protractor to measure each angle. Then, identify each angle as acute, right, or obtuse.

1.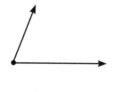

   _____°, _____

2.

   _____°, _____

3.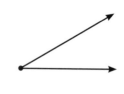

   _____°, _____

4.

   _____°, _____

5.

   _____°, _____

6.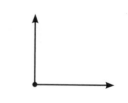

   _____°, _____

7.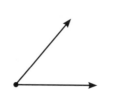

   _____°, _____

8.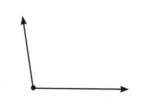

   _____°, _____

9.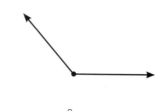

   _____°, _____

Name: _____ Date: _____

Polygons

When three or more line segments come together, they form a **polygon**.

A polygon with 3 sides is a **triangle**

A polygon with 4 sides is a **quadrilateral**.

A polygon with 5 sides is a **pentagon**.

Identify each figure as a triangle, quadrilateral, or pentagon.

1.

_____

2.

_____

3.

_____

4.

_____

5.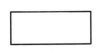

_____

6.

_____

7.

_____

8.

_____

9.

_____

10.

_____

11.

_____

12.

_____

Name: _____   Date: _____

A **polygon** is a closed plane figure formed by three or more line segments.

triangle	**square**	**rectangle**
3 sides	4 sides	4 sides
pentagon	**hexagon**	**octagon**
5 sides	6 sides	8 sides

Draw a line to match each polygon to its name.

1.

                                                 hexagon

2.

                                                 triangle

3.

                                                 square

4.

                                                 rectangle

5.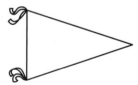

                                                 pentagon

6.

                                                 octagon

Name: _____ Date: _____

Polygons

A **polygon** is a closed plane figure formed by three or more line segments with two sides meeting at each vertex.

 triangle   **quadrilateral**   **square**   **rectangle**   **rhombus**

 parallelogram   **pentagon** **hexagon** **octagon** **trapezoid**

Identify each figure.

1. _____

2. _____

3. _____

4. 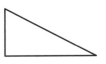 _____

5. _____

6. 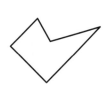 _____

7.  _____

8. 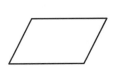 _____

9. _____

10.  _____

11.  _____

12. _____

13. _____

14. _____

15. 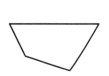 _____

16. _____

Name: _____   Date: _____

Solid Figures

Solid figures are three-dimensional figures. These are common solid figures:

  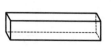

| cube | sphere | rectangular prism | cone | pyramid | cylinder |

Identify each solid figure.

1.

_____

2.

_____

3.

_____

4.

_____

5.

_____

6.

_____

7.

_____

8.

_____

9.

_____

Step Up to Math · Intermediate · CD-104260 · © Carson-Dellosa

Name: _____ Date: _____   115

Solid Figures

Solid figures are three-dimensional figures. These are common solid figures:

| cube | sphere | rectangular prism | cone | pyramid | cylinder |

Identify each solid figure.

1. _____   2. _____   3. _____   4. _____

 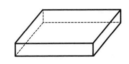

5. _____   6. _____   7. _____   8. _____

9. _____   10. _____   11. _____   12. _____

 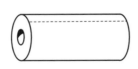 

13. _____   14. _____   15. _____   16. _____

Solid Figures

Solid figures are three-dimensional figures. A flat side of a solid figure is called a **face**.

  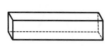

cube	**sphere**	**rectangular prism**	**cone**	**pyramid**	**cylinder**
(6 faces)	(0 faces)	(6 faces)	(1 face)	(5 faces)	(2 faces)

Name the solid figure that each object resembles. Then, write the number of faces it has.

1.

_____

# of faces

2.

_____

# of faces

3.

_____

# of faces

4.

_____

# of faces

5.

_____

# of faces

6.

_____

# of faces

7.

_____

# of faces

8.

_____

# of faces

9.

_____

# of faces

Calculating Perimeter

Perimeter (P) is the total distance around a figure. To find the perimeter, add the lengths of all of the sides.

8 cm

2 cm   2 cm

8 cm

P = 8 cm + 2 cm + 8 cm + 2 cm

P = 20 cm

Find the perimeter of each figure.

1.

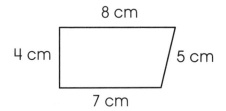

8 cm

4 cm   5 cm

7 cm

P = _____ cm

2.

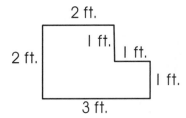

2 ft.

1 ft.

2 ft.   1 ft.

1 ft.

3 ft.

P = _____ ft.

3.

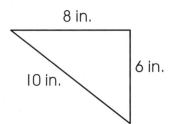

8 in.

6 in.

10 in.

P = _____ in.

4.

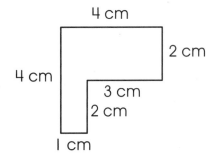

4 cm

2 cm

4 cm

3 cm

2 cm

1 cm

P = _____ cm

5.

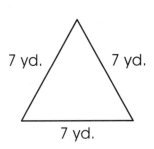

7 yd.   7 yd.

7 yd.

P = _____ yd.

6.

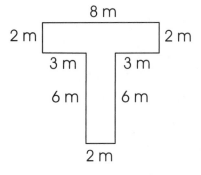

8 m

2 m   2 m

3 m   3 m

6 m   6 m

2 m

P = _____ m

Name: _____ Date: _____

Calculating Perimeter

Perimeter (P) is the total distance around a figure. To find the perimeter, add the lengths of all of the sides.

8 cm

2 cm [rectangle] 2 cm

8 cm

P = 8 cm + 2 cm + 8 cm + 2 cm

P = 20 cm

Find the perimeter of each figure.

1.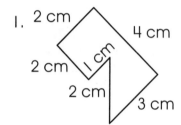
2 cm
4 cm
2 cm   1 cm
2 cm
3 cm

P = _____ cm

2. 1 in.   3 in.
4 in.
3 in.

P = _____ in.

3.
1 cm   2 cm
2 cm   2 cm
2 cm

P = _____ cm

4.
4 in.
1 in.
1 in.   5 in.

P = _____ in.

5.
5 yd.
3 yd. [rectangle] 3 yd.
5 yd.

P = _____ yd.

6.
7 m
2 m [rectangle] 2 m
7 m

P = _____ m

7.
8 in.
5 in.   1 in.
2 in.
4 in.

P = _____ in.

8.
6 cm
4 cm [rectangle] 4 cm
6 cm

P = _____ cm

9.
4 yd.
10 yd. [rectangle] 10 yd.
4 yd.

P = _____ yd.

Name: _____ Date: _____

Calculating Perimeter

Perimeter (P) is the total distance around a figure. To find the perimeter, add the lengths of all of the sides.

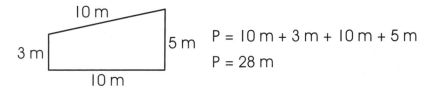

P = 10 m + 3 m + 10 m + 5 m

P = 28 m

Find the perimeter of each figure.

1.

10 in.

6 in. ☐ 6 in.

10 in.

P = _____ in.

2.

5 cm

7 cm / 10 cm

2 cm

P = _____ cm

3.

8 m | 10 m

6 m

P = _____ m

4.

5 ft. 5 ft.

5 ft. 5 ft.

5 ft.

P = _____ ft.

5.

3 cm

8 cm 8 cm

3 cm

P = _____ cm

6.

3 ft.

7 ft. 9 ft.

12 ft.

P = _____ ft.

7.

8 cm

5 cm 8 cm

10 cm

P = _____ cm

8.

3 m 4 m

6 m

6 m 10 m

6 m

P = _____ m

Use a ruler to find the perimeter of each polygon in centimeters.

9.

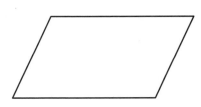

P = _____

10.

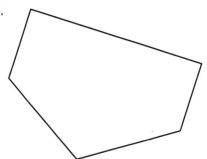

P = _____

Calculating Area

Area is the number of square units inside a figure. Area is measured in units such as square feet (ft.²) or square centimeters (cm²). To find the area, count the number of squares it takes to cover the figure.

There are 6 squares inside the figure, so the area is 6 square units.

Area = 6 square units

Count the squares to find the area of each figure.

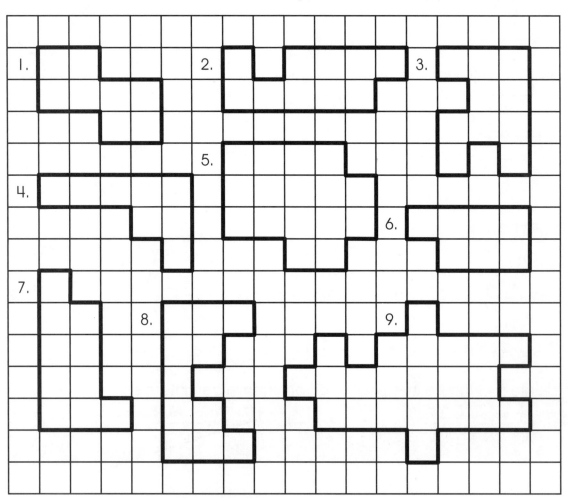

1. Area = _____ cm²   2. Area = _____ cm²   3. Area = _____ cm²

4. Area = _____ cm²   5. Area = _____ cm²   6. Area = _____ cm²

7. Area = _____ cm²   8. Area = _____ cm²   9. Area = _____ cm²

Name: _____ Date: _____

Calculating Area

Area (A) is the number of square units enclosed within a boundary. To find the area of a square or rectangle, multiply the length by the width.

12 cm

4 cm

A = length x width
A = 4 cm x 12 cm
A = 48 cm²

Find the area of each rectangle and square.

1.
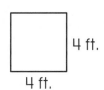
4 ft.
4 ft.

A = _____ ft.²

2.
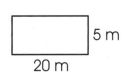
5 m
20 m

A = _____ m²

3.
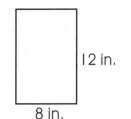
12 in.
8 in.

A = _____ in.²

4.
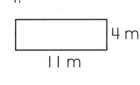
4 m
11 m

A = _____ m²

5.

3 ft.
3 ft.

A = _____ ft.²

6.

8 m
5 m

A = _____ m²

7.
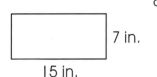
7 in.
15 in.

A = _____ in.²

8.
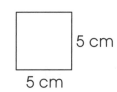
5 cm
5 cm

A = _____ cm²

9.
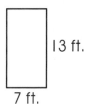
13 ft.
7 ft.

A = _____ ft.²

10.
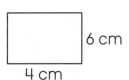
2 cm
12 cm

A = _____ cm²

11.
6 cm
4 cm

A = _____ cm²

12.
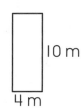
10 m
4 m

A = _____ m²

Name: _____   Date: _____

Calculating Area

Area (A) is the number of square units enclosed within a boundary. To find the area of a right triangle, multiply the base by the height and divide by 2.

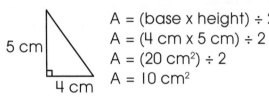

A = (base x height) ÷ 2
A = (4 cm x 5 cm) ÷ 2
A = (20 cm²) ÷ 2
A = 10 cm²

Find the area of each triangle.

1.

A = _____ m²

2.
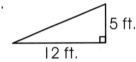

A = _____ ft.²

3.
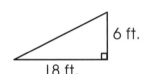

A = _____ ft.²

4.

A = _____ cm²

5.
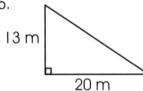

A = _____ m²

6.
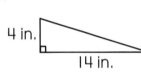

A = _____ in.²

7.
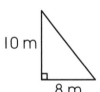

A = _____ m²

8.

A = _____ cm²

Use the measurements provided to find the area of each right triangle. Label your answer.

9. b = 3 in.
   h = 6 in.

10. b = 5 m
    h = 10 m

11. b = 7 ft.
    h = 10 ft.

12. b = 3 mm
    h = 8 mm

A = _____

A = _____

A = _____

A = _____

● ● ●   Step Up to Math   ·   Intermediate   ·   CD-104260   ·   © Carson-Dellosa

Name: _____ Date: _____

Calculating Volume

Volume tells the number of cubic units within a solid figure. Each cube represents one cubic unit. To find volume, count the number of cubes within the figure.

 There are 25 total cubes, so the volume is 25 cubic units.

Volume (V) = 25 cubic units

Find the volume of each figure.

1.

V = _____ cubic units

2.

V = _____ cubic units

3.

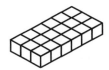

V = _____ cubic units

4.

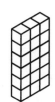

V = _____ cubic units

5.

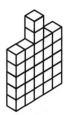

V = _____ cubic units

6.

V = _____ cubic units

Name: _____   Date: _____

Calculating Volume

Volume tells the number of cubic units within a solid figure. To find the volume of a rectangular prism, multiply the length, by the width, by the height (V = l x w x h).

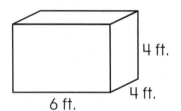

Volume (V) = length x width x height

V = 6 ft. x 4 ft. x 4 ft.

V = 96 ft.³

Find the volume of each figure.

1.

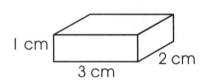

V = _____ cm³

2.

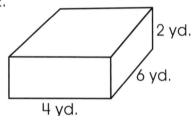

V = _____ yd.³

3.

V = _____ m³

4.

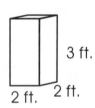

V = _____ ft.³

5.

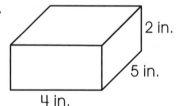

V = _____ in.³

6.

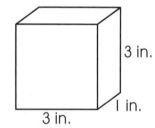

V = _____ in.³

7.

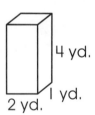

V = _____ yd.³

8.

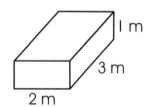

V = _____ m³

9.

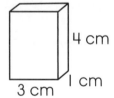

V = _____ cm³

● ●

Name: _____ Date: _____

Calculating Volume

Volume tells the number of cubic units within a solid figure. To find the volume of a rectangular prism, multiply the length, by the width, by the height (V = l x w x h).

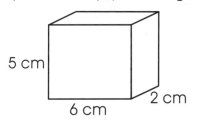

Volume (V) = l x w x h
V = 6 cm x 2 cm x 5 cm
V = 60 cm³

Find the volume of each figure. Label your answer.

1.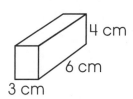

2.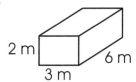

3.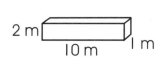

4.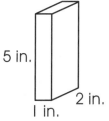

V = _____   V = _____   V = _____   V = _____

5.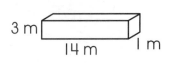

6.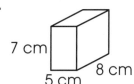

7.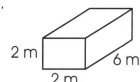

8.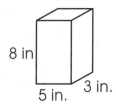

V = _____   V = _____   V = _____   V = _____

Use the given dimensions to find the volume of each rectangular prism. Label your answer.

9. l = 2 cm   10. l = 5 m   11. l = 10 in.   12. l = 3.5 ft.
    w = 4 cm   w = 3 m   w = 3 in.   w = 1 ft.
    h = 3 cm   h = 4 m   h = 5 in.   h = 2 ft.

V = _____   V = _____   V = _____   V = _____

Name: _____ Date: _____

Metric Units of Length

To estimate an object's length, review these metric lengths and their equivalents.

centimeter (cm)   meter (m)   kilometer (km)

100 cm = 1 m

1,000 m = 1 km

Circle the best estimate for the length of each real-life object.

1.

more than 10 centimeters

less than 10 centimeters

2.

more than 5 meters

less than 5 meters

3.

more than 1 meter

less than 1 meter

4.

more than 1 centimeter

less than 1 centimeter

5.

more than 2 meters

less than 2 meters

6.

more than 2 centimeters

less than 2 centimeters

Name: _____ Date: _____

Metric Units of Length

To estimate an object's length, review these metric lengths and their equivalents.

centimeter (cm)   meter (m)   kilometer (km)

100 cm = 1 m

1,000 m = 1 km

Circle the best unit to measure each object.

1. The length of a car.

   A. cm   B. m   C. km

2. The distance from your school to the next closest city.

   A. cm   B. m   C. km

3. The length of a pencil.

   A. cm   B. m   C. km

4. The distance from your school to the zoo.

   A. cm   B. m   C. km

5. The distance from your house to the next closest country.

   A. cm   B. m   C. km

6. The length of a swimming pool.

   A. cm   B. m   C. km

7. The length of your pinky finger.

   A. cm   B. m   C. km

8. The height of a tree.

   A. cm   B. m   C. km

9. The width of a quarter.

   A. cm   B. m   C. km

10. The height of your desk.

   A. cm   B. m   C. km

Name: _____ Date: _____

Metric Units of Length

Review these metric length equivalents:

1 meter (m) = 100 centimeters (cm)

1 kilometer (km) = 1,000 meters (m)

To convert measurements, multiply the measurement by the unit's metric equivalent.

Examples: 3 km = ____ m   Multiply 3 by 1,000   3 km = 3,000 m

            12 m = ____ cm   Multiply 12 by 100   12 m = 1,200 cm

Use the information above to help convert each measurement.

1. 8 km = _____ m   2. 4 km = _____ m

3. 10 km = _____ m   4. 6 km = _____ m

5. 5 m = _____ cm   6. 70 m = _____ cm

7. 2 km = _____ m   8. 9 km = _____ m

9. 7 m = _____ cm   10. 5 m = _____ cm

Write >, <, or = to compare each pair of measurements.

11. 4 m $\bigcirc$ 4 cm   12. 1 km $\bigcirc$ 1,000 m

13. 2 m $\bigcirc$ 200 cm   14. 4 m $\bigcirc$ 50 cm

15. 1 m $\bigcirc$ 150 cm   16. 3 km $\bigcirc$ 3 m

17. 100 m $\bigcirc$ 10 cm   18. 10 km $\bigcirc$ 20 m

19. 30 cm $\bigcirc$ 3 m   20. 5 cm $\bigcirc$ 10 cm

Name: _____ Date: _____

Standard Units of Length

To estimate an object's length, review these standard lengths and their equivalents.

inch (in.)   foot (ft.)   yard (yd.)

12 inches (in.) = 1 foot (ft.)

3 feet (ft.) = 1 yard (yd.)

Circle the best estimate for the length of each real-life object.

1.

more than 1 inch

less than 1 inch

2.

more than 2 inches

less than 2 inches

3.

more than 1 yard

less than 1 yard

4.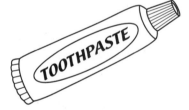

more than 2 feet

less than 2 feet

5.

more than 2 yards

less than 2 yards

6.

more than 2 inches

less than 2 inches

Name: _____ Date: _____

Standard Units of Length

Review these standard length equivalents:

12 inches (in.) = 1 foot (ft.)

3 feet (ft.) = 1 yard (yd.)

5,280 feet (ft.) = 1 mile (mi.)

1,760 yards (yd.) = 1 mile (mi.)

To convert measurements, multiply the measurement by the unit's standard equivalent.

Examples: 3 mi. = _____ yd.   Multiply 3 by 1,760   3 mi. = 5,280 yd.

12 yd. = _____ ft.   Multiply 12 by 3   12 yd. = 36 ft.

Use the information above to help convert each measurement.

1. 3 ft. = _____ in.   2. 3 yd. = _____ ft.   3. 2 mi. = _____ yd.

4. 10 ft. = _____ in.   5. 4 mi. = _____ ft.   6. 5 yd. = _____ ft.

7. 8 ft. = _____ in.   8. 7 ft. = _____ in.   9. 10 yd. = _____ ft.

10. 1 mi. = _____ ft.   11. 2 yd. = _____ ft.   12. 6 yd. = _____ ft.

Circle the most appropriate unit of measure.

13.    14. 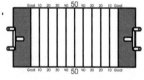   15.    16.

in.   yd.   in.   yd.   in.   mi.   yd.   mi.

17.    18.   19.    20.

mi.   yd.   ft.   yd.   in.   ft.   yd.   mi.

   Step Up to Math · Intermediate · CD-104260 · © Carson-Dellosa

Standard Units of Length

Review these standard length equivalents:

12 inches (in.) = 1 foot (ft.)

3 feet (ft.) = 1 yard (yd.)

5,280 feet (ft.) = 1 mile (mi.)

1,760 yards (yd.) = 1 mile (mi.)

To convert measurements, multiply the measurement by the unit's standard equivalent.

Examples: 3 mi. = _____ yd.   Multiply 3 by 1,760   3 mi. = 5,280 yd.

           12 yd. = _____ ft.   Multiply 12 by 3   12 yd. = 36 ft.

Use the information above to help convert each measurement.

1. 4 ft. = _____ in.

2. 48 in. = _____ ft.

3. 4 yd. = _____ ft.

4. 15 ft. = _____ yd.

5. 2 mi. = _____ yd.

6. 6 yd. = _____ ft.

7. 60 in. = _____ ft.

8. 12 ft. = _____ yd.

9. 30 yd. = _____ ft.

10. 24 ft. = _____ yd.

11. 72 in. = _____ ft.

12. 8 yd. = _____ ft.

Write >, <, or = to compare each pair of measurements.

13. 4 ft. ◯ 2 yd.

14. 1 mi. ◯ 5,280 ft.

15. 18 in. ◯ 1 yd.

16. 2 yd. ◯ 5 ft.

17. 12 ft. ◯ 4 yd.

18. 1 mi. ◯ 1,700 yd.

19. 62 in. ◯ 5 ft.

20. 72 in. ◯ 24 yd.

Name: _____   Date: _____

Measuring Temperature

Temperatures can be measured using either side of a thermometer. One side measures in **Fahrenheit** (°F), which is the standard unit of measure. The other side measures in **Celsius** (°C), which is the metric unit of measure.

To find the temperature, trace a line with your finger from the top of the temperature bar to the measurement line beside the temperature. Count each measurement line as one degree.

Examples:

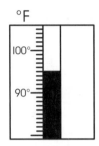

This thermometer reads 95°F   This thermometer reads 3°C

Find each temperature in degrees Fahrenheit.

1.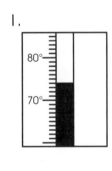

_____°F

2.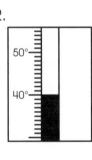

_____°F

3.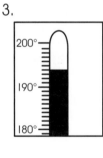

_____°F

4.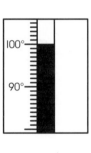

_____°F

5.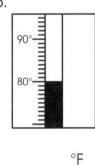

_____°F

Find each temperature in degrees Celsius.

6.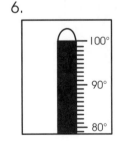

_____°C

7.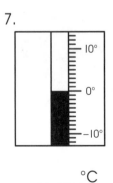

_____°C

8.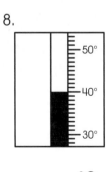

_____°C

9.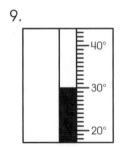

_____°C

10.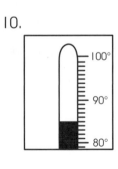

_____°C

Name: _____   Date: _____

Measuring Temperature

Temperatures can be measured using either side of a thermometer. One side measures in **Fahrenheit** (°F), which is the standard unit of measure. The other side measures in **Celsius** (°C), which is the metric unit of measure.

To find the temperature in degrees Fahrenheit, trace a line with your finger from the top of the temperature bar to the measurement line beside the temperature. Count each Fahrenheit measurement line as two degrees.

To estimate degrees Celsius, trace a line with your finger from the top of the temperature bar to the nearest measurement line beside the temperature. Count each Celsius measurement line as one degree.

Example: The thermometer to the right reads 88°F and is approximately 31°C.

Find each temperature in degrees Fahrenheit. Then, estimate each temperature in degrees Celsius.

1.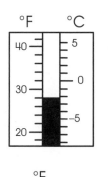

_____ °F   _____ °C

2.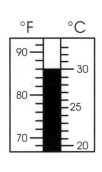

_____ °F   _____ °C

3.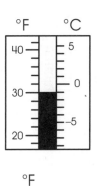

_____ °F   _____ °C

4.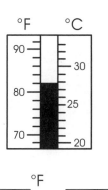

_____ °F   _____ °C

5.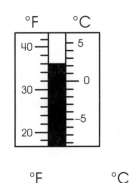

_____ °F   _____ °C

6.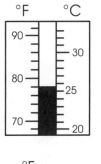

_____ °F   _____ °C

Name: _____ Date: _____

Measuring Temperature

Temperatures can be measured using either side of a thermometer. One side measures in **Fahrenheit** (°F), which is the standard unit of measure. The other side measures in **Celsius** (°C), which is the metric unit of measure.

Use the given temperature movement to find each new temperature.

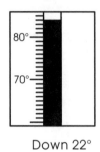   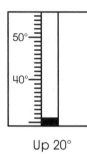   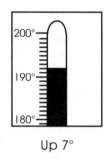   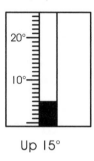   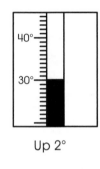

Down 22°   Up 20°   Up 7°   Up 15°   Up 2°

1. _____°F   2. _____°F   3. _____°F   4. _____°F   5. _____°F

Use the given temperature movement to find each new temperature.

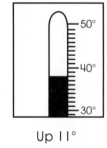   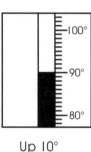   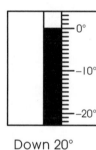   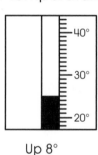

Up 11°   Up 10°   Down 20°   Up 8°   Up 15°

6. _____°C   7. _____°C   8. _____°C   9. _____°C   10. _____°C

Answer the questions.

11. If the normal human body temperature is 98.6°F, how much cooler is the temperature of water freezing (32°F)? _____

12. What is the difference in temperature between water boiling (212°F) and water freezing (32°F)? _____

13. What is the difference in temperature between water boiling (100°C) and water freezing (0°C)? _____

14. What is the difference in temperature between water boiling (100°C) and the normal human body temperature (37°C) ?

_____

Name: _____   Date: _____

Pictographs and Bar Graphs

Bar graphs can be used to display and compare information. The bar graph below shows the results of a science experiment to find the best plant food.

Use the bar graph below to answer each question.

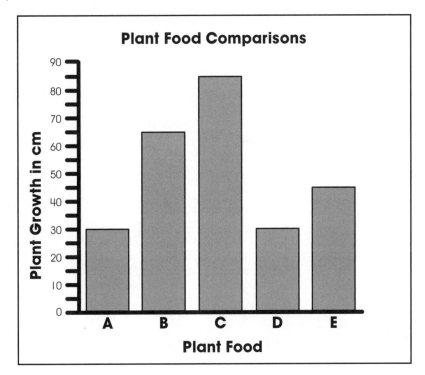

1. How much did the plant that received Food B grow? _____

2. Which two plant foods produced the same growth?
   _____ and _____

3. How much more did the plant that received Food C grow than the plant that received Food A? _____

4. How much did the plant that received Food E grow? _____

5. Which two plant foods produced 110 cm of growth altogether?
   _____ and _____

6. How much more did the plant that received Food B grow than the plant that received Food D? _____

Name: _____ Date: _____

Pictographs and Bar Graphs

Pictographs use pictures to display and compare information. The pictograph below shows the results of a food drive at Lindy Elementary School.

Use the pictograph to answer each question.

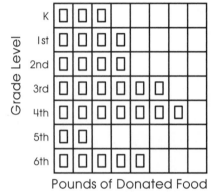

Lindy Elementary Food Drive

Each ☐ stands for 60 pounds of donated food.

1. Which grade level donated the most pounds of food?_____

2. Which grade level donated 120 pounds of food? _____

3. What was the total amount of food donated by the entire school?

    _____

4. How many more pounds of food did the 4th grade donate than the 5th grade?

    _____

5. Who donated more food, the 1st grade or the 6th grade? _____

6. How many more pounds of food did the kindergarten donate than the
    5th grade? _____

7. Which grade level donated a total of 300 pounds of food? _____

8. How many pounds of food did the 3rd grade and the 4th grade
    donate altogether? _____

Name: _____ Date: _____

Pictographs and Bar Graphs

Pictographs use pictures to compare information. **Bar graphs** use bars to compare information.

The Favorite Frozen Fruit Treats pictograph below shows the type of frozen treats eaten at Armstrong Elementary. The Food Bank Volunteers bar graph shows the number of volunteers at two different schools.

Use the graphs to answer each question.

Favorite Frozen Fruit Treats at Armstrong Elementary

Type of Frozen Treat					
Grape	⊸▭	⊸▭	⊸◿		
Orange	⊸▭	⊸▭	⊸◿		
Cranberry	⊸▭	⊸▭	⊸▭		
Cherry	⊸▭	⊸▭	⊸▭	⊸▭	
Strawberry	⊸▭	⊸▭	⊸▭	⊸▭	⊸▭
Kiwi	⊸▭	⊸▭	⊸▭		
Apple	⊸▭				

Number of Frozen Treats Eaten

⊸▭ = 12 frozen fruit treats

⊸◿ = 6 frozen fruit treats

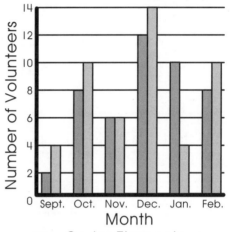

Food Bank Volunteers

◼ = Carter Elementary

◻ = Madison Elementary

1. Which flavor was the most popular?

   _____

2. Which two flavors were half as popular as the most popular choice?

   _____

   _____

3. Which flavor was the least popular?

   _____

4. Which flavor was the second most popular?

   _____

5. Which school had more volunteers in December?

   _____

6. What was the total number of volunteers at that school for December?

   _____

7. How many more volunteers helped from Carter Elementary than from Madison Elementary during January?

   _____

8. Which school had more volunteers in October?

   _____

Name: _____ Date: _____

Circle Graphs and Line Graphs

Circle graphs are divided into parts to display and compare information.
Line graphs are used to show how information changes over time.

The circle graph below shows the results of a survey. The line graph below shows the number of movie tickets sold during a five-day period.

Use the circle graph to answer each question.

Favorite Activities

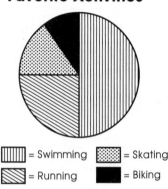

| = Swimming | = Skating |
| = Running | = Biking |

1. What is the most popular activity?

   _____

2. What is the least popular activity?

   _____

3. Do students prefer running or biking more?

   _____

4. Do students prefer skating or biking more? _____

5. Do students prefer running or skating more? _____

Use the line graph to answer each question.

6. How many tickets were sold on Wednesday?

   _____

7. How many tickets were sold on Monday?

   _____

8. Were more tickets sold on Thursday or Friday?

   _____

9. On what day were the most tickets sold? _____

10. On what day were the least tickets sold? _____

Name: _____ Date: _____ 139

Circle Graphs and Line Graphs

Circle graphs are divided into parts to display and compare information.
Line graphs are used to show how information changes over time.

The circle graph below shows the results of a survey. The line graph below shows the number of babysitting jobs Eva had during a seven-month period.

Use the graphs to answer each question.

Favorite Vegetables

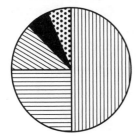

 = Broccoli   = Tomatoes

= Yellow Squash   ■ = Beets

= Peas

Eva's Babysitting Jobs

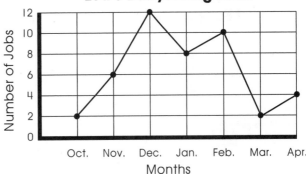

1. Which two vegetables are the least favorite?

    _____

2. Which vegetable is the favorite?

    _____

3. Which vegetable is liked half as much as broccoli?

    _____

4. Which vegetable is liked more, peas or tomatoes?

    _____

5. In what month did Eva have the most babysitting jobs?

    _____

6. Between which two months was the greatest decrease in the number of babysitting jobs?

    _____

7. Between which two months was the greatest increase in the number of babysitting jobs?

    _____

8. What was the total number of babysitting jobs Eva had from the beginning of October to the end of December?

    _____

Name: _____ Date: _____

Circle Graphs and Line Graphs

Circle graphs are divided into parts to display and compare information. A complete circle graph represents 100% of the information. **Line graphs** are used to show how information changes over time.

The circle graph below shows the results of a survey. The line graph below shows how attendance changed during a six-week period.

Use the graphs to answer each question.

Favorite Flower Colors

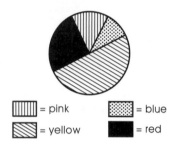

▥ = pink   ⬚ = blue
▨ = yellow   ■ = red

Singing Club Attendance

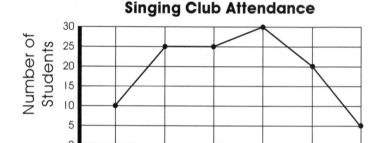

1. Which color is the most popular?

   _____

2. Which color is the least popular?

   _____

3. Which color is half as popular as the most popular color?

   _____

4. Which two colors, when combined, equal the amount of popularity of the color red?

   _____

5. What percent of the circle graph do the four colors make altogether?

   _____

6. Which week had the highest attendance?

   _____

7. Between which two weeks was the greatest decrease in attendance?

   _____

8. Between which two weeks was the greatest increase in attendance?

   _____

9. How many students attended Singing Club in the 3rd week?

   _____

10. Which week had the lowest attendance?

   _____

Using a Diagram

Sometimes, a diagram and the information within it can be used to solve problems.

Use the diagram below to answer the questions about Mrs. April's classroom.

1. How many desks are in the classroom? _____

2. What is the area of Kenny's desk? _____ ft.²

3. What is the area of Amy's desk? _____ ft.²

4. What is the area of the fish tank? _____ ft.²

5. What is the area of the closet? _____ ft.²

6. What is the area of the bookcase? _____ ft.²

7. How many square feet do the closet and the bookcase total? _____ ft.²

8. What is the area of the computer center? _____ ft.²

9. What is the area of the art corner? _____ ft.²

10. How much larger in area is the computer center than the bookcase? _____ ft.²

Mrs. April's Classroom
(all measurements shown in feet)

Name: _____ Date: _____

Using a Diagram

Sometimes, a diagram and the information within it can be used to solve problems.

Use the diagram below to answer the questions about Pat's bedroom.

1. How many desks are in the bedroom? _____
2. What is the area of the computer desk? _____ ft.²
3. What is the area of the bed? _____ ft.²
4. What is the area of the fish tank? _____ ft.²
5. What is the area of the closet? _____ ft.²
6. What is the area of the bookcase? _____ ft.²
7. How many square feet do the closet and the bookcase total? _____ ft.²
8. How many square feet do the bed and the desk total? _____ ft.²
9. How much larger in area is the computer desk than the desk? _____ ft.²
10. What is the area of the table? _____ ft.²

Pat's Bedroom
(all measurements shown in feet)

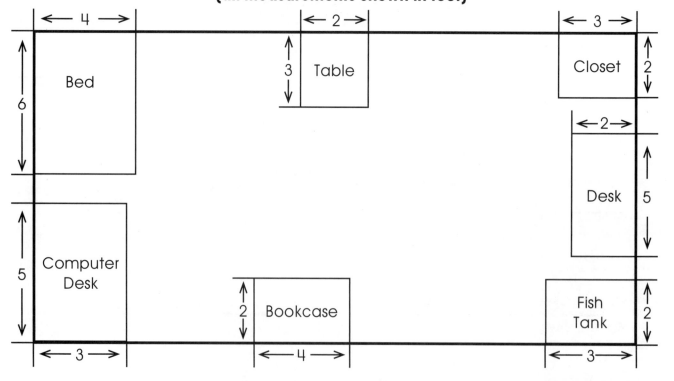

Name: _____   Date: _____   143

Using a Diagram

Sometimes, a diagram and the information within it can be used to solve problems.

Use the diagram below to answer the questions about the Wong family's house.

Second Floor of the Wong's House

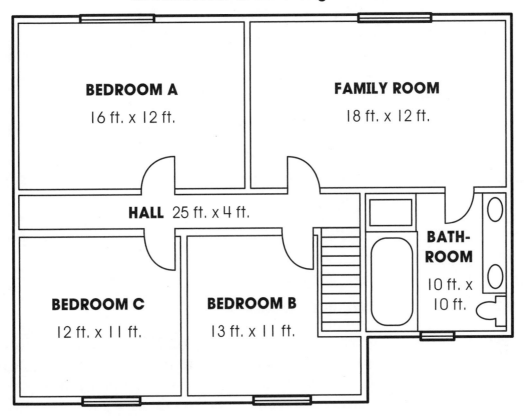

1. What is the area of the family room? _____ ft.²

2. How much larger in area is the family room than bedroom C? _____ ft.²

3. How many square feet do the three bedrooms total? _____ ft.²

4. What is the area of the bathroom? _____ ft.²

5. What is the total area of the entire upstairs? _____ ft.²

6. What is the difference in area between the largest bedroom and

    the bathroom? _____ ft.²

Using a Tree Diagram

A **tree diagram** shows all of the outcomes or combinations for a situation.

Example: Tyler wants to buy a sundae, but he cannot decide between the hot fudge and the strawberry toppings. He also has a choice of three extra toppings: colorful sprinkles, chocolate candies, or crushed cookies. How many different choices does Tyler have?

List the topping choices. Then, list the extra toppings. Draw a line from each topping choice to all of the extra toppings.

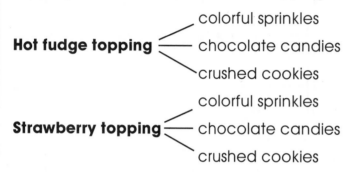

Hot fudge topping
- colorful sprinkles
- chocolate candies
- crushed cookies

Strawberry topping
- colorful sprinkles
- chocolate candies
- crushed cookies

Then, count all of the choices in the last row for the answer. Tyler has six choices to choose between.

Draw a tree diagram to solve each problem.

1. Nikki wants to plant flowers. She must choose between roses, daffodils, and carnations. She must also choose whether to plant the flowers in pots or in hanging baskets. How many choices does she have altogether?

2. Mike is taking a band class. He gets to learn either the clarinet or the trumpet. He must also choose between marching band and concert band. How many choices does Mike have?

Name: _____   Date: _____

Using a Tree Diagram

A **tree diagram** shows all of the outcomes or combinations for a situation.

Example: Tammy and Debbie want to order potatoes. The restaurant gives a choice of a red potato or a brown potato. The potato can be served three different ways: mashed, baked, or as french fries. How many different choices are there?

List the potato choices. Then, list the ways that it can be served. Draw a line from each potato to all of the serving types.

red potato ⟨ mashed baked french fries   brown potato ⟨ mashed baked french fries

There are three choices for the red potato, and three choices for the brown potato. There are six total choices.

Draw a tree diagram to solve each problem.

1. David wants to buy a new bike. He can buy a mountain bike, a road bike, or a racing bike. The store has each of these bikes in a choice of red, blue, or purple. How many choices does he have in all?

2. Elaine is at the school picnic. She can choose between a hot dog or a hamburger. She must also choose whether to get chips, fruit, or a salad. How many choices does Elaine have?

3. Carlos wants a new pair of shoes. He can choose between running shoes, walking shoes, or basketball shoes. He must also choose between black, red, or white shoes. How many choices does Carlos have?

Using a Tree Diagram

A **tree diagram** shows all of the outcomes or combinations for an event or situation.

Draw a tree diagram to solve each problem.

1. Gwen has Saturday and Sunday free, so she is planning her weekend. Each day, she must choose between reading, swimming, miniature golfing, or horseback riding. How many choices does she have for the weekend?

2. Eric needs to buy a new bike helmet. He has two basic choices. There is a new streamline helmet, or the basic helmet. Both helmets come in purple or blue. They also come in small, medium, and large sizes. How many choices does Eric have?

3. Juanita wants a new paintbrush for art class. At the store, she sees that there are stiff bristles and soft bristles. Also, there are long brushes and short brushes. Lastly, there are wide, medium, and narrow brushes. How many choices does Juanita have?

Name: _____ Date: _____ 147

Using A Table

A **table** uses numbers rather than pictures to provide information.

Lauren's Lunch Menu

Lunch Items	Price
Chicken Nuggets	$2.75
Hamburger	$2.50
Hot Dog	$2.25
Carrots	$0.50
Fresh Fruit	$0.65
Juice	$1.00
Water	$0.75

Use the table to answer each question.

1. The Owen family has $10.00. Do they have enough money to buy 4 hamburgers?

    _____

2. James would like a hot dog, carrots, and juice. What is the total cost?

    _____

3. Lynn bought 1 hot dog using a $5 bill. How much change will she get?

    _____

4. How much will 5 waters cost?

    _____

5. Tammy and Tara each want chicken nuggets and water. How much will their lunches cost altogether?

    _____

6. Max has $2.00. Can he buy fresh fruit, carrots, and juice?

    _____

7. What is the difference between the price of chicken nuggets and the price of 1 hot dog?

    _____

8. Harry wants to buy 1 hot dog and 1 water. What will his lunch cost?

    _____

Using A Table

A **table** uses numbers rather than pictures to provide information.

Sam's Market

Fruit	Fruit Prices
Fresh Cherries	$2.99 per lb.
Red Delicious Apples	$0.89 per lb.
Green Grapes	$1.49 per lb.
Strawberries	$3.49 per basket
Bananas	$0.59 per lb.
Pineapples	$1.99 each

Use the table to answer each question.

1. José wants to buy 1 pound of green grapes and a pineapple. He only has $5.00. Can he purchase these two items?

   _____

2. Jennifer wants to buy 3 pounds of fresh cherries. What will her total cost be?

   _____

3. Jeremy needs 1 basket of strawberries, 1 pineapple, and 1 pound of fresh cherries to make a fruit salad. What will his total cost be?

   _____

4. Alecia wants to buy 1 basket of strawberries and 1 pound of bananas, or 1 pound of fresh cherries and 1 pound of green grapes? Which combination will be less expensive?

   _____

5. Anna spent $4.47 buying three pounds of fruit. Which type of fruit did she buy?

   _____

6. David wants to purchase 1 pound of red delicious apples and 1 pound of bananas. What will he pay altogether?

   _____

7. Andy has 6 quarters. Does he have enough money to purchase 1 pineapple?

   _____

Name: _____   Date: _____

Using A Table

A **table** uses numbers rather than pictures to provide information.

Flour Needed for Monica's Famous Baked Dishes

Dish	Amount of Flour
Baked Chicken and Vegetables	$2\frac{1}{2}$ cups
Baked Zucchini Sticks with Onions	$1\frac{3}{4}$ cups
Baked Sausage and Peppers	$3\frac{1}{8}$ cups
Chicken Stew and Dumplings	$2\frac{1}{4}$ cups
Turkey Potpie	$4\frac{1}{8}$ cups
Wheat Germ Blueberry Muffins	$2\frac{3}{4}$ cups

Use the table to answer each question. Show your work in the space provided.

1. How much more flour is needed to make turkey potpie than baked zucchini sticks with onions? _____ cups

2. How much flour is needed altogether to make baked sausage and peppers and baked chicken and vegetables? _____ cups

3. Which takes more flour to bake, turkey potpie or wheat germ blueberry muffins?

   _____

4. How much less flour is needed to make chicken stew and dumplings than baked sausage and peppers? _____ cups

5. How much total flour is needed to make baked sausage and peppers, turkey potpie, and wheat germ blueberry muffins? _____ cups

Name: _____ Date: _____

Coordinate Graphs

A **grid** can be used to show an object's location. It has numbered or lettered lines.

Example: To find the location of the 🌸 , move along the bottom horizontal line and find the lettered line the flower is on. Then, move up the line vertically and trace across to see what numbered line it is on. This flower is located at (F, 3).

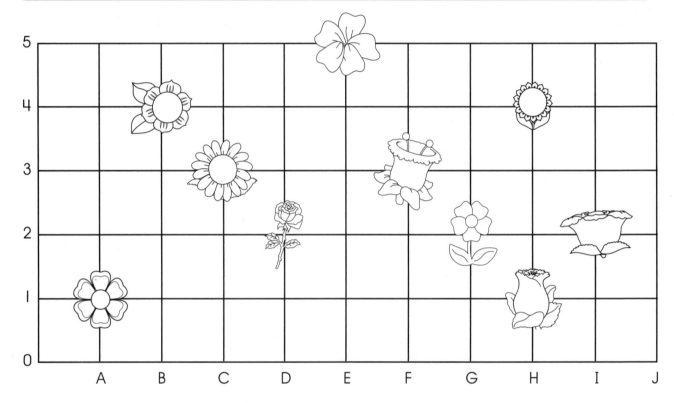

Use the grid above to write the location of each plant.

1. = (____ , ____) 2. = (____ , ____) 3. = (____ , ____)

4. = (____ , ____) 5. = (____ , ____) 6. = (____ , ____)

7. = (____ , ____) 8. = (____ , ____) 9. = (____ , ____)

● **Step Up to Math** · **Intermediate** · **CD-104260** · © Carson-Dellosa

Coordinate Graphs

An **ordered pair** can be used to locate a point on a grid or coordinate graph. It looks like this: (2, 3). The first number tells how many units the point is to the right of zero. The second number tells how many units the point is located up from zero.

Example: Find (2, 3). Move right 2, and up 3.

What is the secret message? Write the letters in order on the lines provided for each ordered pair.

1. (4, 6) _____
2. (7, 7) _____
3. (5, 1) _____
4. (1, 1) _____

5. (1, 1) _____
6. (1, 4) _____
7. (6, 2) _____
8. (4, 3) _____
9. (0, 5) _____

10. (8, 3) _____
11. (2, 7) _____
12. (6, 5) _____
13. (3, 2) _____
14. (1, 4) _____
15. (5, 1) _____

16. (5, 1) _____
17. (1, 1) _____
18. (1, 4) _____
19. (4, 3) _____
20. (2, 7) _____
21. (2, 4) _____
22. (8, 1) _____
23. (5, 1) _____
24. (7, 4) _____

Name: _____ Date: _____

Coordinate Graphs

An **ordered pair** can be used to locate a point on a grid or coordinate graph. It looks like this: (2, 4). The first number tells how many units the point is to the right of zero. The second number tells how many units the point is located up from zero.

Example: Find (2, 4). Move right 2, and up 4.

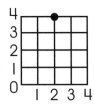

Write the letters for each ordered pair to find the message.

___ ___ ___ ___   ___ ___   ___ ___ ___   ___ ___   ___ ___ ___
(2, 1) (4, 5) (1, 3) (8, 3)   (1, 0) (4, 1)   (5, 4) (7, 1) (1, 5)   (5, 4) (4, 3)   (1, 3) (8, 3) (1, 5)

___ ___ ___ ___ ___ ___ ___ ___ ___ ___   ___ ___ ___
(1, 0) (7, 1) (7, 4) (5, 1) (1, 5) (6, 6) (1, 0) (1, 5) (7, 1) (1, 3) (4, 1)   (4, 3) (5, 4) (5, 1)

___ ___ ___ ___ ___ ___
(2, 1) (4, 5) (6, 3) (1, 0) (7, 1) (7, 4)

___ ___ ___ ___   ___ ___ ___ ___
(1, 2) (1, 0) (4, 3) (1, 5)   (4, 3) (3, 3) (7, 1) (6, 2)

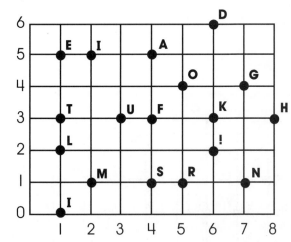

Page 6

1. top left wing: blue, bottom left wing: orange, top right wing: green, bottom right wing: yellow, body: red; 2. forty-two thousand one hundred sixty-three; 3. 31,421; 4. 61,564; 5. ninety-seven thousand three hundred fifty-eight

Page 7

1. 5, 2, 3, 1, 8, 6; 2. 0, 8, 9, 2, 0, 7; 3. 8, 3, 4, 6, 5, 1; 4. ten thousands; 5. thousands; 6. tens; 7. hundred thousands; 8. hundreds; 9. ones; 10. ten thousands

Page 8

1. 40,000; 2. 8,000,000,000; 3. 50,000,000; 4. 5,000; 5. 8; 6. 70,000; 7. 3,000,000; 8. 400,000; 9. 700,000,000; 10. 2,000,000,000; 11. 6; 12. 200; 13. three billion four hundred twenty-one million eight hundred thousand; 14. forty-five billion nine hundred eighty-two million four hundred six thousand three hundred ninety-nine

Page 9

1. 700; 2. 100; 3. 600; 4. 300; 5. 700; 6. 900; 7. 700; 8. 500; 9. 900

Page 10

1. 70; 2. 60; 3. 10; 4. 60; 5. 80; 6. 20; 7. 50; 8. 30; 9. 300; 10. 900; 11. 600; 12. 400; 13. 800; 14. 700; 15. 700; 16. 200; 17. 1,000; 18. 2,000 19. 1,000; 20. 4,000; 21. 6,000; 22. 8,000; 23. 10,000; 24. 4,000; 25. 6,000

Page 11

1. 8,000; 2. 9,000; 3. 1,000; 4. 3,000; 5. 7,000; 6. 8,000; 7. 5,000; 8. 10,000; 9. 6,000; 10. 7,000; 11. 60,000; 12. 50,000; 13. 80,000; 14. 40,000; 15. 30,000; 16. 20,000; 17. 40,000; 18. 80,000; 19. 60,000; 20. 70,000; 21. 2,000,000; 22. 3,000,000; 23. 7,000,000; 24. 5,000,000; 25. 6,000,000; 26. 2,000,000

Page 12

1. <; 2. <; 3. >; 4. >; 5. <; 6. >; 7. >; 8. <; 9. <; 10. >

Page 13

1. <; 2. >; 3. <; 4. <; 5. >; 6. =; 7. >; 8. <; 9. >; 10. >; 11. =; 12. <; 13. <; 14. >; 15. <; 16. <; 17. <; 18. >

Page 14

1. <; 2. =; 3. <; 4. >; 5. <; 6. <; 7. >; 8. <; 9. >; 10. =; 11. <; 12. <; 13. 1,400,892; 1,408,241; 9,426,597; 14. 328,191; 340,384; 342,192; 15. 65,382; 68,297; 405,495; 929,058

Page 15

1. 85; 2. 82; 3. 90; 4. 68; 5. 31; 6. 50; 7. 635; 8. 777; 9. 949; 10. 817; 11. 368; 12. 576; 13. 212; 14. 397; 15. 974

Page 16

1. 13,368; 2. 8,272; 3. 11,386; 4. 9,299; 5. 9,413; 6. 9,501; 7. 10,144; 8. 13,719; 9. 9,065; 10. 6,452; 11. 8,629; 12. 6,680; 13. 59,613; 14. 100,997; 15. 112,615; 16. 106,135

Page 17

1. 8,730; 2. 7,821; 3. 10,623; 4. 4,415; 5. 64,802; 6. 5,546; 7. 46,073; 8. 43,563; 9. 58,621; 10. 96,442; 11. 62,343; 12. 73,332; 13. 81,530; 14. 106,008; 15. 51,474; 16. 93,477

Page 18

1. 256; 2. 667; 3. 215; 4. 174; 5. 406; 6. 27; 7. 195; 8. 254; 9. 383; 10. 389; 11. 366; 12. 499; 13. 352; 14. 235; 15. 194

Page 19

1. 258; 2. 256; 3. 126; 4. 264; 5. 177; 6. 488; 7. 758; 8. 3,596; 9. 4,387; 10. 1,463; 11. 8,918; 12. 1,886; 13. 1,689; 14. 1,778; 15. 1,889; 16. 3,856

Page 20

1. 11,908; 2. 13,136; 3. 24,825; 4. 24,133; 5. 5,816; 6. 21,916; 7. 11,583; 8. 27,915; 9. 61,378; 10. 17,947; 11. 29,106; 12. 28,092; 13. 30,909; 14. 24,105; 15. 31,787; 16. 15,863

Page 21

1. 13; 2. 21; 3. 21; 4. 24; 5. 8; 6. 16; 7. 11; 8. 12; 9. 42; 10. 12; 11. 2; 12. 15; 13. 33; 14. 25; 15. 25; 16. 41; 17. 33; 18. 48; 19. 36; 20. 12

Page 22

1. 366; 2. 401; 3. 122; 4. 576; 5. 173; 6. 244; 7. 1,764; 8. 2,047; 9. 6,722; 10. 519; 11. 2,853; 12. 8,719; 13. 4,109; 14. 2,916; 15. 7,884; 16. 3,393

Page 23

1. 892; 2. 2,973; 3. 8,272; 4. 2,352; 5. 4,253; 6. 2,054;
7. 959; 8. 975; 9. 88,795; 10. 4,132; 11. 97,211;
12. 12,223; 13. 15,156; 14. 12,092; 15. 31,765;
16. 481,884

Page 24

1. 850; 2. 360; 3. 660; 4. 380; 5. 170; 6. 490; 7. 880;
8. 140; 9. 710; 10. 820; 11. 650; 12. 280; 14. 930;
14. 330; 15; 860; 16. 220; 17. 460; 18; 700; 19. 870;
20. 640

Page 25

1. 64,200; 2. 32,300; 3. 49,600; 4. 16,500; 5. 64,900;
6. 87,400; 7. 94,000; 8. 52,800; 9. 80,500; 10. 76,400;
11. 21,400; 12. 29,500; 13. 83,000; 14. 38,400;
15. 90,300; 16. 47,200; 17. 38,100; 18. 16,800;
19. 24,700; 20. 68,700

Page 26

1. 165,000; 2. 982,000; 3. 756,000; 4. 240,000;
5. 452,000; 6. 598,000; 7. 265,000; 8. 422,000;
9. 326,000; 10. 584,000; 11. 649,000; 12. 467,000;
13. 687,000; 14. 806,000; 15. 256,000; 16. 590,000;
17. 238,000; 18. 198,000; 19. 201,000; 20. 485,000

Page 27

1. 282; 2. 168; 3. 324; 4. 185; 5. 472; 6. 64; 7. 84;
8. 504; 9. 215; 10. 144; 11. 204; 12. 282; 13. 602;
14. 290; 15. 376; 16. 86; 17. 186; 18. 192; 19. 128;
20. 147

Page 28

1. 642; 2. 568; 3. 2,550; 4. 972; 5. 1,048; 6. 738;
7. 2,056; 8. 1,491; 9. 3,708; 10. 2,526; 11. 1,770;
12. 1,008; 13. 2,448; 14. 711; 15. 2,172; 16. 1,970;
17. 840; 18. 7,767; 19. 2,274; 20. 6,818

Page 29

1. 9,369; 2. 8,486; 3. 25,926; 4. 4,912; 5. 11,008;
6. 22,615; 7. 16,926; 8. 25,281; 9. 30,834; 10. 14,061;
11. 18,728; 12. 32,291; 13. 8,529; 14. 22,280;
15. 9,726; 16. 22,520

Page 30

1. 630; 2. 880; 3. 810; 4. 2,280; 5. 1,150; 6. 920;
7. 1,500; 8. 1,120; 9. 560; 10. 2,070; 11. 2,520;
12. 1,040; 13. 1,120; 14. 3,560; 15. 1,260

Page 31

1. 1,312; 2. 840; 3. 714; 4. 672; 5. 1,092; 6. 7,316;
7. 5,275; 8. 5,760; 9. 10,208; 10. 4,878; 11. 17,465;
12. 10,295; 13. 18,576; 14. 3,757; 15. 19,600;

Page 32

1. 55,440; 2. 154,420; 3. 38,136; 4. 222,220; 5. 35,489;
6. 114,546; 7. 222,955; 8. 188,244; 9. 97,848;
10. 96,764; 11. 232,705; 12. 147,614

Page 33

1. 86,700; 2. 129,600; 3. 27,000; 4. 330,000;
5. 279,200; 6. 44,100; 7. 179,000; 8. 215,400

Page 34

1. 43,680; 2. 94,500; 3. 123,900; 4. 322,080;
5. 205,000; 6. 64,080; 7. 166,820; 8. 42,560; 9. 63,000;
10. 391,730; 11. 82,600; 12. 177,840

Page 35

1. 38,745; 2. 73,986; 3. 147,136; 4. 100,890;
5. 126,236; 6. 79,356; 7. 206,625; 8. 78,474;
9. 261,330; 10. 92,127; 11. 74,169; 12. 140,544;
13. 203,184; 14. 61,712; 15. 142,780

Page 36

1. 2; 2. 5; 3. 2; 4. 4; 5. 3; 6. 5; 7. 2; 8. 6; 9. 2; 10. 5;
11. 2; 12. 5

Page 37

1. 2; 2. 6; 3. 8; 4. 4; 5. 3; 6. 3; 7. 6; 8. 3; 9. 5; 10. 3;
11. 3; 12. 5; 13. 3; 14. 4; 15. 9; 16. 9; 17. 7; 18. 9;
19. 8; 20. 7

Page 38

1. 6; 2. 1; 3. 5; 4. 8; 5. 7; 6. 9; 7. 10; 8. 2; 9. 4; 10. 3;
A SWIFTWALKER

Page 39

1. 22; 2. 49; 3. 18; 4. 12; 5. 15; 6. 29; 7. 12; 8. 38;
9. 14; 10. 18; 11. 24; 12. 17

Page 40

1. 21; 2. 32; 3. 21; 4. 34; 5. 13; 6. 18; 7. 25; 8. 13;
9. 17; 10. 12; 11. 16; 12. 28; 13. 19; 14. 12; 15. 12;
16. 38

Page 41

1. 98; 2. 67; 3. 68; 4. 91; 5. 34; 6. 78; 7. 26; 8. 73;
9. 58; 10. 81; 11. 96; 12. 47; 13. 29; 14. 48; 15. 27;
16. 29

Page 42

1. 4 R2; 2. 6 R2; 3. 9 R4; 4. 5 R2; 5. 3 R2; 6. 8 R2;
7. 7 R5; 8. 9 R2; 9. 6 R3; 10. 4 R3; 11. 4 R4; 12. 9 R7;
13. 5 R6; 14. 3 R5; 15. 6 R6; 16. 3 R3

Page 43

1. 5 R2; 2. 8 R1; 3. 4 R1; 4. 3 R2; 5. 4 R3; 6. 9 R3;
7. 6 R3; 8. 2 R4; 9. 9 R3; 10. 3 R3; 11. 5 R5; 12. 8 R3;
13. 3 R4; 14. 5 R5; 15. 6 R2; 16. 5 R2

Page 44

1. 59 R1; 2. 56 R3; 3. 88 R4; 4. 112 R1; 5. 74 R1;
6. 94 R2; 7. 96 R7; 8. 41 R5; 9. 24 R1; 10. 83 R3;
11. 173 R1; 12. 75 R5

Page 45

1. 29 R2; 2. 19 R2; 3. 48 R1; 4. 11 R5; 5. 13 R3;
6. 25 R2; 7. 35 R1; 8. 15 R1; 9. 14 R1; 10. 19 R3;
11. 22 R2; 12. 24 R1

Page 46

1. 13 R2; 2. 11 R4; 3. 35 R1; 4. 11 R3; 5. 22 R3;
6. 22 R1; 7. 46 R1; 8. 15 R2; 9. 122 R6; 10. 132 R2;
11. 158 R2; 12. 135 R6

Page 47

1. 79 R1; 2. 58 R3; 3. 42 R4; 4. 63 R7; 5. 28 R4;
6. 39 R3; 7. 27 R4; 8. 96 R2; 9. 72 R3; 10. 28 R5;
11. 78 R6; 12. 97 R1

Page 48

1. 100; 2. 50; 3. 90; 4. 50; 5. 90; 6. 90; 7. 30; 8. 60;
9. 60; 10. 50; 11. 80; 12. 40

Page 49

1. 308 R1; 2. 180 R4; 3. 406 R1; 4. 209 R3; 5. 140 R5;
6. 109 R2; 7. 120 R6; 8. 108 R2; 9. 340 R1; 10. 190 R2;
11. 405 R1; 12. 103 R4

Page 50

1. 50 R3; 2. 402 R2; 3. 800 R1; 4. 109 R1; 5. 405 R1;
6. 103 R4; 7. 30 R8; 8. 309 R4; 9. 706 R2; 10. 205 R5;
11. 907 R3; 12. 108 R2

Page 51

1. 5; 2. 4; 3. 5; 4. 10; 5. 9; 6. 4; 7. 8; 8. 8; 9. 4; 10. 10;
11. 5; 12. 5; 13. 2; 14. 7; 15. 7

Page 52

1. 14 R18; 2. 34 R16; 3. 23 R5; 4. 17 R8; 5. 37 R16;
6. 32 R28; 7. 21 R32; 8. 14 R16; 9. 31 R35; 10. 13 R42;
11. 41 R7; 12. 21 R34

Page 53

1. 430 R9; 2. 56 R6; 3. 299 R13; 4. 38 R38; 5. 14 R21;
6. 36 R20; 7. 28 R40; 8. 21 R50; 9. 370 R4

Page 54

1. $\frac{4}{6}$; 2. $\frac{1}{3}$; 3. $\frac{2}{3}$; 4. $\frac{1}{4}$; 5. $\frac{1}{3}$; 6. $\frac{2}{4}$; 7. $\frac{3}{6}$; 8. $\frac{3}{8}$;
9. $\frac{2}{4}$; 10. $\frac{1}{2}$; 11. $\frac{1}{4}$; 12. $\frac{2}{6}$; 13. $\frac{3}{4}$; 14. $\frac{6}{12}$; 15. $\frac{5}{15}$

Page 55

1. 7; 2. 3; 3. 6; 4. 9; 5. 5; 6. 5; 7. 4; 8. 3; 9. 7; 10. 3;
11. 7; 12. 9

Page 56

1. 5; 2. 2; 3. 5; 4. 5; 5. 2; 6. 3; 7. 4; 8. 9; 9. 6; 10. 5;
11. 9; 12. 2; 13. 9; 14. 7; 15. 2; 16. 2

Page 57

1. $\frac{1}{3} = \frac{2}{6}$; 2. $\frac{1}{4} = \frac{2}{8}$; 3. $\frac{1}{2} = \frac{3}{6}$; 4. $\frac{3}{4} = \frac{6}{8}$; 5. $\frac{2}{2} = \frac{1}{1}$;
6. $\frac{3}{7} = \frac{6}{14}$; 7. $\frac{1}{5} = \frac{2}{10}$; 8. $\frac{1}{6} = \frac{2}{12}$; 9. $\frac{8}{8} = \frac{1}{1}$; 10. $\frac{2}{3} = \frac{6}{9}$;
11. $\frac{2}{4} = \frac{8}{16}$; 12. $\frac{1}{4} = \frac{3}{12}$

Page 58

1. $\frac{5}{10}$, $\frac{2}{10}$, 10; 2. $\frac{3}{6}$, $\frac{2}{6}$, 6; 3. $\frac{8}{24}$, $\frac{3}{24}$, 24; 4. $\frac{7}{14}$, $\frac{2}{14}$, 14;
5. $\frac{4}{12}$, $\frac{3}{12}$, 12; 6. $\frac{9}{18}$, $\frac{2}{18}$, 18

Page 59

1. $\frac{3}{12}$, $\frac{2}{12}$, 12; 2. $\frac{7}{21}$, $\frac{3}{21}$, 21; 3. $\frac{6}{30}$, $\frac{5}{30}$, 30; 4. $\frac{7}{42}$, $\frac{6}{42}$, 42;
5. $\frac{7}{28}$, $\frac{4}{28}$, 28; 6. $\frac{5}{15}$, $\frac{3}{15}$, 15

Page 60

1. $\frac{1}{2}$; 2. $\frac{2}{5}$; 3. $\frac{2}{3}$; 4. $\frac{1}{3}$; 5. $\frac{2}{3}$; 6. $\frac{7}{9}$

Page 61

1. $\frac{5}{6}$; 2. $\frac{1}{4}$; 3. $\frac{1}{3}$; 4. $\frac{1}{3}$; 5. $\frac{7}{8}$; 6. $\frac{1}{5}$; 7. $\frac{1}{3}$; 8. $\frac{1}{5}$; 9. $\frac{1}{2}$

Page 62

1. $\frac{1}{3}$; 2. $\frac{4}{13}$; 3. $\frac{5}{8}$; 4. $\frac{6}{7}$; 5. $\frac{1}{5}$; 6. $\frac{5}{18}$; 7. $\frac{3}{8}$; 8. $\frac{1}{6}$;
9. $\frac{2}{5}$; 10. $\frac{1}{5}$; 11. $\frac{2}{9}$; 12. $\frac{1}{11}$

Page 63

1. $\frac{3}{4}$; 2. $\frac{1}{4}$; 3. $\frac{4}{5}$; 4. $\frac{9}{10}$; 5. $\frac{1}{4}$; 6. $\frac{3}{5}$; 7. $\frac{8}{9}$; 8. $\frac{1}{3}$;
9. $\frac{2}{5}$; 10. $\frac{4}{5}$; 11. $\frac{2}{5}$; 12. $\frac{1}{5}$

Answer Key

Page 64
1. $\frac{1}{7}$; 2. $\frac{7}{9}$; 3. $\frac{9}{14}$; 4. $\frac{1}{5}$; 5. $\frac{9}{11}$; 6. $\frac{3}{4}$; 7. $\frac{1}{5}$; 8. $\frac{1}{3}$;
9. $\frac{2}{5}$; 10. $\frac{3}{13}$; 11. $\frac{1}{4}$; 12. $\frac{2}{5}$

Page 65
1. $\frac{7}{8}$; 2. $\frac{1}{2}$; 3. $\frac{1}{2}$; 4. $\frac{10}{11}$; 5. $\frac{1}{12}$; 6. $\frac{7}{8}$; 7. $\frac{2}{13}$; 8. $\frac{1}{9}$;
9. $\frac{2}{15}$; 10. $\frac{11}{12}$; 11. $\frac{11}{12}$; 12. $\frac{9}{10}$

Page 66
1. $\frac{1}{3} < \frac{2}{3}$; 2. $\frac{2}{4} = \frac{4}{8}$; 3. $\frac{3}{8} < \frac{1}{2}$; 4. $\frac{1}{3} = \frac{2}{6}$; 5. $\frac{3}{4} > \frac{2}{4}$;
6. $\frac{1}{2} < \frac{3}{4}$

Page 67
1. >; 2. <; 3. >; 4. =; 5. <; 6. >; 7. =; 8. <; 9. <; 10. <;
11. <; 12. >; 13. <; 14. =; 15. >

Page 68
1. <; 2. <; 3. <; 4. <; 5. =; 6. <; 7. >; 8. <; 9. >; 10. <;
11. <; 12. =; 13. >; 14. <; 15. >; 16. <; 17. <; 18. >

Page 69
1. $2\frac{1}{7}$; 2. $3\frac{1}{2}$; 3. $2\frac{1}{3}$; 4. $2\frac{1}{5}$; 5. $1\frac{8}{9}$; 6. $3\frac{1}{4}$;
7. $3\frac{1}{5}$; 8. $5\frac{1}{2}$; 9. $2\frac{1}{2}$; 10. $4\frac{1}{5}$; 11. $3\frac{5}{6}$; 12. $3\frac{1}{6}$;
13. $4\frac{1}{2}$; 14. $2\frac{1}{2}$; 15. $4\frac{1}{3}$; 16. $2\frac{1}{4}$

Page 70
1. $4\frac{4}{5}$; 2. $9\frac{4}{5}$; 3. $9\frac{9}{14}$; 4. $6\frac{1}{2}$; 5. $11\frac{5}{12}$; 6. $3\frac{3}{8}$;
7. $9\frac{2}{9}$; 8. $7\frac{1}{6}$; 9. $13\frac{2}{5}$; 10. $4\frac{1}{2}$; 11. $8\frac{2}{15}$; 12. $6\frac{1}{12}$

Page 71
1. $2\frac{5}{8}$; 2. $4\frac{3}{5}$; 3. $3\frac{3}{10}$; 4. 9; 5. $5\frac{8}{9}$; 6. $4\frac{3}{4}$; 7. $4\frac{5}{18}$;
8. 5; 9. $3\frac{9}{10}$; 10. $1\frac{9}{14}$; 11. 4; 12. $1\frac{7}{12}$

Page 72
1. 8.6; 2. 5.8; 3. 7.4; 4. 4.4; 5. three and seven
tenths; 6. four and three tenths; 7. seven and two
tenths; 8. eight and nine tenths; 9. two and one
tenth

Page 73
1. $\frac{2}{5}$, 0.4; 2. $\frac{1}{5}$, 0.2; 3. $\frac{1}{2}$, 0.5; 4. $1\frac{2}{5}$, 1.4;
5. $1\frac{1}{10}$, 1.1; 6. $1\frac{9}{10}$, 1.9

Page 74
1. 3.5; 2. 6.1; 3. 0.8; 4. 8.3; 5. 0.3; 6. 2.1; 7. 0.7;
8. 20.2; 9. 0.4; 10. 7.2; 11. three and nine tenths;
12. two and seven tenths; 13. twelve and eight
tenths; 14. seven and three tenths; 15. five tenths;
16. one and one tenth; 17. six and four tenths;
18. two and six tenths; 19. four and two tenths;
20. four and four tenths; 21. $\frac{3}{5}$; 22. $\frac{1}{2}$; 23. $\frac{9}{10}$; 4. $\frac{7}{10}$;
25. $1\frac{1}{5}$; 26. $4\frac{4}{5}$

Page 75
1. 2.65; 2. 2.42; 3. four and thirty-one hundredths;
4. seven and twenty-six hundredths; 5. eight and
nine hundredths; 6. forty-three hundredths;
7. six and seventy-three hundredths

Page 76
1. $\frac{21}{100}$, 0.21; 2. $\frac{47}{100}$, 0.47; 3. $\frac{17}{50}$, 0.34;
4. $\frac{69}{100}$, 0.69; 5. $1\frac{7}{100}$, 1.07; 6. $1\frac{1}{50}$, 1.02

Page 77
1. 9.16; 2. 14.72; 3. 200.34; 4. 47.89; 5. 11.62;
6. $\frac{2}{25}$; 7. $6\frac{9}{100}$; 8. $2\frac{3}{25}$; 9. $\frac{21}{100}$; 10. $7\frac{17}{50}$; 11. $\frac{11}{20}$;
12. $16\frac{2}{25}$; 13. $300\frac{6}{25}$; 14. $25\frac{1}{25}$; 15. $600\frac{49}{100}$;
16. $\frac{18}{25}$; 17. $\frac{11}{50}$; 18. $25\frac{17}{50}$; 19. $9\frac{9}{100}$; 20. $4\frac{39}{100}$

Page 78
1. 6; 2. 4; 3. 4; 4. 0; 5. 5; 6. 1; 7. 3; 8. 2; 9. 5; 10. 3;
11. 9; 12. 2; 13. 0.241; 14. 0.004; 15. 0.150;
16. 0.922; 17. 0.815; 18. 0.005; 19. 0.351;
20. 0.100

Page 79
1. 0.425; 2. 0.126; 3. 0.900; 4. 0.778; 5. 0.236;
6. 0.649; 7. 0.518; 8. 0.002; 9. 0.586; 10. 0.927;
11. nine, thirty-four; 12. two; 13. three, fifty; 14. nine,
twenty-five; 15. one, ninety-four; 16. nine,
seventy-three; 17. four, twenty-nine; 18. four,
eighty-six; 19. nine, seventy-one; 20. fifty-two

Page 80
1. 0.307; 2. 15.045; 3. 0.218; 4. 0.002;
5. thirty-five thousandths; 6. eighty-nine and
four thousandths; 7. eighteen and four hundred
twenty-seven thousandths; 8. $\frac{237}{1,000}$; 9. $6\frac{259}{1,000}$;
10. $2\frac{633}{1,000}$; 11. $\frac{651}{1,000}$; 12. $7\frac{529}{1,000}$; 13. $\frac{981}{1,000}$;
14. $1\frac{253}{1,000}$; 15. $8\frac{779}{1,000}$; 16. $\frac{437}{1,000}$

Page 81

1. 0.5, 1.5, 2.5, 3.5; 2. 4.5, 5.5, 6.5, 7.5; 3. 0.5, 1.0, 1.5, 2.0; 4. 1.5, 2.0, 2.5, 3.0; 5. 0.5, 2.5, 3.0, 3.5; 6. 2.5, 3.5, 4.0, 4.5, 5.0

Page 82

1. >; 2. <; 3. >; 4. <; 5. <; 6. <; 7. >; 8. >; 9. >; 10. >; 11. <; 12. >; 13. <; 14. <; 15. <

Page 83

1. <; 2. >; 3. <; 4. >; 5. >; 6. <; 7. =; 8. >; 9. >; 10. <; 11. =; 12. >; 13. >; 14. <; 15. <; 16. >; 17. >; 18. <

Page 84

1. 6; 2. 25; 3. 4; 4. 3; 5. 10; 6. 9; 7. 5; 8. 113; 9. 7; 10. 18; 11. 15; 12. 29; 13. $4.00; 14. $11.00; 15. $9.00; 16. $21.00; 17. $8.00; 18. $8.00; 19. $9.00; 20. $10.00; 21. $6.00; 22. $10.00; 23. $11.00; 24. $14.00

Page 85

1. 46; 2. 3; 3. 612; 4. 346; 5. 7; 6. 1; 7. 88; 8. 44; 9. 4.4; 10. 2.9; 11. 543.2; 12. 56.1; 13. 3.2; 14. 78.1; 15. 0.4; 16. 36.2; 17. $35.00; 18. $26.00; 19. $64.00; 20. $23.00; 21. $39.00; 22. $24.00; 23. $13.00; 24. $29.00

Page 86

1. 15; 2. 4; 3. 57; 4. 723; 5. 38; 6. 624; 7. 19; 8. 78; 9. 56.3; 10. 10.9; 11. 41.1; 12. 132.8; 13. 18.8; 14. 5.4; 15. 307.7; 16. 60.4; 17. 230.04; 18. 0.30; 19. 155.87; 20. 59.31; 21. 35.51; 22. 158.34; 23. 725.98; 24. 82.36

Page 87

1. 4.2; 2. 9.6; 3. 4.3; 4. 8.2; 5. 4.14; 6. 9.77; 7. 9.45; 8. 8.2; 9. 8.8; 10. 7.7; 11. 9.50; 12. 7.84; 13. 2.54; 14. 7.82; 15. 9.1; 16. 7.6

Page 88

1. 25.63; 2. 40.5; 3. 52.7; 4. 89.5; 5. 94.64; 6. 88.0; 7. 8.34; 8. 46.27; 9. 19.33; 10. 68.61; 11. 55.59; 12. 64.93; 13. 74.49; 14. 12.91; 15. 68.73

Page 89

1. 346.24; 2. 0.661; 3. 8.555; 4. 24.116; 5. 51.24; 6. 16.157; 7. 9.65; 8. 19.245; 9. 32.352; 10. 25.555; 11. 26.638; 12. 13.04; 13. 83.056; 14. 25.254

Page 90

1. 2.6; 2. 3.8; 3. 2.74; 4. 3.0; 5. 3.18; 6. 9.41; 7. 6.21; 8. 6.4; 9. 1.5; 10. 4.1; 11. 5.18; 12. 4.22; 13. 2.22; 14. 2.16; 15. 8.7

Page 91

1. 11.7; 2. 1.43; 3. 13.92; 4. 8.68; 5. 22.2; 6. 3.13; 7. 34.46; 8. 23.33; 9. 22.1; 10. 21.29; 11. 1.61; 12. 26.67; 13. 1.12; 14. 3.3; 15. 12.33; 16. 17.92; 17. 40.47; 18. 3.70; 19. 3.67; 20. 1.19

Page 92

1. 26.061; 2. 23.276; 3. 13.547; 4. 18.632; 5. 14.122; 6. 14.80; 7. 36.08; 8. 1.427; 9. 25.285; 10. 33.14; 11. 1.66; 12. 43.735; 13. 11.334; 14. 12.218; 15. 32.483; 16. 12.465; 17. 11.804; 18. 25.869; 19. 22.198; 20. 2.367

Page 93

1. $35.00; 2. $32.00; 3. $24.00; 4. $42.00; 5. $18.00; 6. $4.00; 7. $18.00; 8. $10.00; 9. $7.00; 10. $63.00; 11. $24.00; 12. $27.00; 13. $48.00; 14. $9.00; 15. $16.00; 16. $42.00

Page 94

1. $7.23; 2. $23.34; 3. $0.84; 4. $192.96; 5. $2.52; 6. $46.23; 7. $29.47; 8. $3.70; 9. $10.29; 10. $314.50; 11. $45.36; 12. $136.64; 13. $89.04; 14. $11.96; 15. $640.90; 16. $219.70

Page 95

1. $78.24; 2. $1,429.68; 3. $2,116.46; 4. $2,229.12; 5. $318.06; 6. $139.65; 7. $269.12; 8. $225.92; 9. $1,608.75; 10. $655.64; 11. $47.04; 12. $44.84; 13. $131.22; 14. $731.12; 15. $197.34; 16. $797.64

Page 96

1. $2.00; 2. $3.00; 3. $2.00; 4. $3.00; 5. $1.00; 6. $3.00; 7. $5.00; 8. $5.00; 9. $1.00

Page 97

1. $3.24; 2. $2.23; 3. $1.27; 4. $1.14; 5. $2.16; 6. $2.18; 7. $1.13; 8. $2.36; 9. $1.08; 10. $1.24; 11. $2.19; 12. $1.84

Page 98

1. $5.48; 2. $0.78; 3. $6.21; 4. $3.59; 5. $6.24; 6. $1.05; 7. $7.12; 8. $3.79; 9. $5.88; 10. $1.87; 11. $4.11; 12. $3.56; 13. $0.76; 14. $3.89; 15. $1.47; 16. $6.21

Page 99

1. C.; 2. A.; 3. B.; 4. B.

Answer Key

Page 100

1.
2.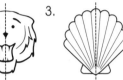
3.

4.
5.
6.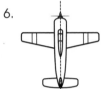

7.
8.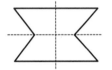

9.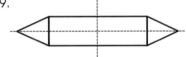

Page 101

1. yes; 2. yes; 3. yes; 4. no; 5. yes; 6. yes; 7. no;
8. no; 9. yes; 10. no; 11. yes; 12. yes; 13. yes; 14. yes;
15. no;

16.
17.

18.
19.
20.

Page 102

1. =
2. 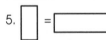 =

3. = 4. = 5.  =

6. = 7.  =

Page 102 (continued)

8. = 9. =

10. =

Page 103

1. flip; 2. similar; 3. turn; 4. slide; 5. similar; 6. flip

Page 104

1.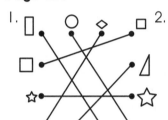
2.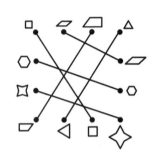

3.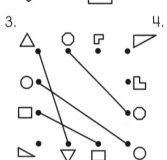
4.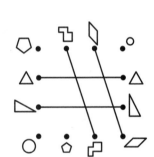

Page 105

1. line segment; 2. line segment; 3. line; 4. ray;
5. line; 6. line segment; 7. ray CD; 8. line RS or SR;
9. ray EF; 10. line segment YZ or ZY; 11. line UV or
VU; 12. line segment NO or ON

Page 106

1. $\overrightarrow{CD}$; 2. $\overleftrightarrow{CM}$ or $\overleftrightarrow{MC}$; 3. $\overline{XY}$ or $\overline{YX}$; 4. $\overleftrightarrow{AB}$ or $\overleftrightarrow{BA}$;
5. $\overrightarrow{BC}$ or $\overrightarrow{CB}$; 6. $\overleftrightarrow{ST}$ or $\overleftrightarrow{TS}$; 7. $\overline{EF}$; 8. $\overrightarrow{DE}$; 9. $\overleftrightarrow{YZ}$ or $\overleftrightarrow{ZY}$;
10. intersecting lines; 11. parallel lines;
12. perpendicular lines

Page 107

1. $\overleftrightarrow{MN}$ or $\overleftrightarrow{NM}$; 2. $\overrightarrow{ST}$; 3. $\overline{UV}$ or $\overline{VU}$; 4. perpendicular
lines; 5. intersecting lines; 6. parallel lines; 7. false;
8. false; 9. true; 10. false

Page 108

1. acute; 2. acute; 3. obtuse; 4. right; 5. obtuse;
6. right; 7. obtuse; 8. acute; 9. obtuse

Page 109

1. acute; 2. right; 3. obtuse; 4. right; 5. obtuse;
6. acute; 7. obtuse; 8. right; 9. acute; 10. obtuse;
11. acute; 12. obtuse

Page 110

1. 70°, acute; 2. 170°, obtuse; 3. 30°, acute;
4. 10°, acute; 5. 120°, obtuse; 6. 90°, right;
7. 50°, acute; 8. 100°, obtuse; 9. 130°, obtuse

Page 111

1. quadrilateral; 2. triangle; 3. triangle;
4. pentagon; 5. quadrilateral; 6. triangle;
7. pentagon; 8. pentagon; 9. quadrilateral;
10. triangle; 11. quadrilateral; 12. pentagon

Page 112

1. rectangle; 2. octagon; 3. pentagon; 4. square;
5. triangle; 6. hexagon

Page 113

Answers will vary but may include: 1. rhombus,
quadrilateral, or parallelogram; 2. octagon;
3. quadrilateral or trapezoid; 4. triangle;
5. square, rectangle, rhombus, parallelogram,
or quadrilateral; 6. pentagon; 7. rectangle,
quadrilateral, or parallelogram; 8. rhombus,
parallelogram, or quadrilateral; 9. hexagon;
10. triangle; 11. quadrilateral; 12. parallelogram
or quadrilateral; 13. rectangle, quadrilateral, or
parallelogram; 14. pentagon; 15. quadrilateral;
16. square, rectangle, rhombus, parallelogram,
or quadrilateral

Page 114

1. rectangular prism; 2. pyramid; 3. sphere;
4. cone; 5. cube; 6. cylinder; 7. pyramid;
8. cylinder; 9. cube

Page 115

1. pyramid; 2. cylinder; 3. sphere; 4. cone;
5. cube; 6. rectangular prism; 7. pyramid;
8. sphere; 9. cylinder; 10. pyramid; 11. cube;
12. cube; 13. cone; 14. cylinder; 15. sphere;
16. cylinder

Page 116

1. cone, 1; 2. cylinder, 2; 3. sphere, 0; 4. cube, 6;
5. pyramid, 5; 6. cube, 6; 7. cone, 1; 8. sphere, 0;
9. cube, 6

Page 117

1. 24; 2. 10; 3. 24; 4. 16; 5. 21; 6. 32

Page 118

1. 14; 2. 11; 3. 9; 4. 11; 5. 16; 6. 18; 7. 20; 8. 20; 9. 28

Page 119

1. 32; 2. 24; 3. 24; 4. 25; 5. 22; 6. 31; 7. 31; 8. 29;
9. 13 cm; 10. 15 cm

Page 120

1. 8; 2. 10; 3. 10; 4. 8; 5. 16; 6. 7; 7. 10; 8. 11; 9. 22

Page 121

1. 16; 2. 100; 3. 96; 4. 44; 5. 9; 6. 40; 7. 105; 8. 25;
9. 91; 10. 24; 11. 24; 12. 40

Page 122

1. 12; 2. 30; 3. 54; 4. 105; 5. 130; 6. 28; 7. 40; 8. 120;
9. 9 in.²; 10. 25 m²; 11. 35 ft.²; 12. 12 mm²

Page 123

1. 20; 2. 12; 3. 18; 4. 18; 5. 27; 6. 20

Page 124

1. 6; 2. 48; 3. 4; 4. 12; 5. 40; 6. 9; 7. 8; 8. 6; 9. 12

Page 125

1. 72 cm³; 2. 36 m³; 3. 20 m³; 4. 10 in.³; 5. 42 m³;
6. 280 cm³; 7. 24 m³; 8. 120 in.³; 9. 24 cm³; 10. 60 m³;
11. 150 in.³; 12. 7 ft.³

Page 126

1. less than 10 centimeters; 2. less than 5 meters;
3. less than 1 meter; 4. more than 1 centimeter;
5. more than 2 meters; 6. more than 2 centimeters

Page 127

1. B.; 2. C.; 3. A.; 4. C.; 5. C.; 6. B.; 7. A.; 8. B.; 9. A.;
10. B.

Page 128

1. 8,000; 2. 4,000; 3. 10,000; 4. 6,000; 5. 500; 6. 7,000;
7. 2,000; 8. 9,000; 9. 700; 10. 500; 11. >; 12. =; 13. =;
14. >; 15. <; 16. >; 17. >; 18. >; 19. <; 20. <

Answer Key

Page 129

1. less than 1 inch; 2. less than 2 inches; 3. less than 1 yard; 4. less than 2 feet; 5. more than 2 yards; 6. more than 2 inches

Page 130

1. 36; 2. 9; 3. 3,520; 4. 120; 5. 21,120; 6. 15; 7. 96; 8. 84; 9. 30; 10. 5,280; 11. 6; 12. 18; 13. in.; 14. yd.; 15. in.; 16. mi.; 17. yd.; 18. ft.; 19. in.; 20. yd.

Page 131

1. 48; 2. 4; 3. 12; 4. 5; 5. 3,520; 6. 18; 7. 5; 8. 4; 9. 90; 10. 8; 11. 6; 12. 24; 13. <; 14. =; 15. <; 16. >; 17. =; 18. >; 19. >; 20. <

Page 132

1. 74; 2. 40; 3. 194; 4. 100; 5. 80; 6. 100; 7. 0; 8. 40; 9. 30; 10. 85

Page 133

1. 28, −2; 2. 86, 30; 3. 30, −1; 4. 82, 28; 5. 36, 2; 6. 78, 26

Page 134

1. 62; 2. 51; 3. 199; 4. 20; 5. 32; 6. 49; 7. 100; 8. −20; 9. 33; 10. 80; 11. 66.6°F; 12. 180°F; 13. 100°C; 14. 63°C

Page 135

1. 65 cm; 2. Food A, Food D; 3. 55 cm; 4. 45 cm; 5. Food B, Food E; 6. 35 cm

Page 136

1. 4th grade; 2. 5th grade; 3. 1,860 pounds; 4. 300 pounds; 5. 6th grade; 6. 60 pounds; 7. 6th grade; 8. 780 pounds

Page 137

1. strawberry; 2. grape and orange; 3. apple; 4. cherry; 5. Madison Elementary; 6. 14 volunteers; 7. 6 more; 8. Madison Elementary

Page 138

1. swimming; 2. biking; 3. running; 4. skating; 5. running; 6. 30 tickets; 7. 10 tickets; 8. Friday; 9. Friday; 10. Monday

Page 139

1. beets and peas; 2. broccoli; 3. yellow squash; 4. tomatoes; 5. December; 6. February and March; 7. November and December; 8. 20 jobs

Page 140

1. yellow; 2. blue; 3. red; 4. pink and blue; 5. 100%; 6. the 4th week; 7. the 5th and 6th weeks; 8. the 1st and 2nd weeks; 9. 25 students; 10. the 6th week

Page 141

1. 2 desks; 2. 15; 3. 12; 4. 6; 5. 6; 6. 10; 7. 16; 8. 20; 9. 20; 10. 10

Page 142

1. 2 desks; 2. 15; 3. 24; 4. 6; 5. 6; 6. 8; 7. 14; 8. 34; 9. 5; 10. 6

Page 143

1. 216; 2. 84; 3. 467; 4. 100; 5. 883; 6. 92

Page 144

1. 6 choices; 2. 4 choices

Page 145

1. 9 choices; 2. 6 choices; 3. 9 choices

Page 146

1. 8 choices; 2. 12 choices; 3. 12 choices

Page 147

1. yes; 2. $3.75; 3. $2.75; 4. $3.75; 5. $7.00; 6. no; 7. $0.50; 8. $3.00

Page 148

1. yes; 2. $8.97; 3. $8.47; 4. 1 basket of strawberries and 1 pound of bananas; 5. green grapes; 6. $1.48; 7. no

Page 149

1. $2\frac{3}{8}$; 2. $5\frac{5}{8}$; 3. turkey pot pie; 4. $\frac{7}{8}$; 5. 10

Page 150

1. (D, 2); 2. (E, 5); 3. (H, 4); 4. (H, 1); 5. (C, 3); 6. (I, 2); 7. (B, 4); 8. (G, 2); 9. (A, 1)

Page 151

MATH HELPS YOU GET THE POINT!

Page 152

MATH IS ONE OF THE INGREDIENTS FOR MAKING LIFE FUN!